Spartan Mental Toughness

Train Your Mind to Sidestep Mental Resistance, Power Through Discomfort, and Ignore Distraction to Achieve the Goals You Truly Want and Others Dream Of. Even Beginners Can Learn These Brain-training Secrets.

Leo Black

Table of Contents

Introduction

"What a disgrace it is to see a man grow old without ever seeing the beauty and strength of which he is capable." - Unknown

You're at your desk, hard at work on a project. Your phone buzzes. It's a text message from your girlfriend or a Facebook notification or a reminder that your phone has a low battery. How long does it take you to get back to work? 20 minutes? 30? An hour?

Perhaps your concentration is fine on a good day, but the moment something goes wrong in your life, you find yourself unable to perform the simplest tasks.

Maybe you're strong and capable when you're confident, but you fall apart in uncomfortable situations, inevitably making things worse.

Maybe you're afraid to take the risks you need to take to get what you want out of life, because you know you'll just get in your own way and screw everything up.

If this sounds like you, then you're in good company. Feelings of distraction, fear, and awkwardness plague every human at one time or another. The few individuals who manage to keep their cool in tough situations or remain focused in the face of distractions aren't superhuman. They aren't psychologically or emotionally superior, and they certainly weren't born that way. What they've done is mastered the art of mental toughness.

Sometimes called mental "resilience," mental toughness isn't about shutting down your feelings or feeling no fear. Mentally tough people get distracted, too. They often feel helpless, afraid, or anxious around others. The difference, however, is that they know how to handle these feelings and still maintain control over their own mind. Mental toughness won't stop you from feeling nervous in social settings or starting to daydream around three in the afternoon. What it *will* do is give you the tools to overcome the mental and emotional cues that stop you from being the person that you want to be.

Mental toughness will help you still be the life of the party when you feel nervous in social settings. It will help you to regain focus when you start to drift off, to let go of distractions, and to face life's challenges without emotionally falling apart.

Mental toughness is about taking back control of your own mind. Your thoughts and feelings don't have to be chaotic. Our contemporary world is full of distractions. From social media to text messaging to the easy availability of media like music, movies, and videos, there's a lot out there to stop us from focusing on the things that are most important. The ability to focus, to think creatively and innovatively, and to face difficult feelings like fear and anger are…well, abilities. They're skills like any other, skills that anyone can master with the proper amount of training and practice. They aren't personality traits.

You don't have to be scatterbrained or forgetful if you don't want to be. You don't have to be too anxious to ask someone you like out on a date or too stressed to search for a better job. You have the power to achieve anything that you want to achieve, and be anyone you want to be. The true obstacles to be faced aren't out in the world; they're within your own mind. The biggest obstacle in your way of being who you want to be is your mindset.

Consider this book a training manual for your mind. It will help you to cultivate heightened mental resilience in the face of any and all adversity. The techniques and philosophies presented in this book are validated by modern psychology, but they are hardly modern ideas. In fact, they're quite ancient, coming to us from the ancient Greek city-state of Sparta. Known and respected for their prowess in battle, the Spartans were a tough lot. Their culture was built on deep values of glory and humility, but also on savagery and pain. The Spartans developed a unique cultural mindset, a certain combination of mental characteristics that helped them to endure even the toughest of life's challenges.

Today's world is very different from ancient Sparta, but the way the human mind works hasn't changed at all. You may not be heading off to battle or protecting your land from wild animals, but you face your own set of challenges every day. You face the social, mental, and emotional pressures of paying rent, meeting deadlines, and managing abusive bosses and difficult coworkers. You face the challenge of staying focused with your phone constantly ringing in your pocket, and feeling secure with access to the world's worst news 24/7. You face the challenges that come with online dating. You manage to pay student loans, utilities, and regularly shop for groceries working a minimum wage job. Your life may look very different from the life of a Spartan, but you and they still live in human societies that are fraught with mental and emotional danger. Though we face different challenges today, we have a great deal to learn from the Spartan mindset. The mental and emotional strategies they developed to become the most respected warrior culture in the ancient Mediterranean can be applied today to help us face the challenges of modern life.

By studying the Spartan philosophy and pairing it with contemporary psychological knowledge, you can become just as mental resilient as any Spartan warrior. This book will walk you through ancient philosophies and modern techniques for maintaining focus, thinking creatively, and mastering emotions that once seemed paralyzing.

In this book, I will guide you through the basics of the Spartan mindset, and pair the ancient social guidelines with modern psychological studies. This book will also provide you with a number of practice techniques that you can apply to your own life. Many of the exercises in this book will seem difficult, strange, and uncomfortable at first. That's ok—it's part of the process. But with time, you'll begin to feel yourself growing mentally stronger. As you build up your mental resilience, you'll find yourself more and more empowered to achieve your goals and get the things that you want out of life. Mental resilience is the key to success. With it, there will be no challenge too difficult for you to overcome, no obstacle big enough to stop you from living the life you want to live. With this book in hand, you will have all the tools that you need to become the master of your own mind, and by extension, the master of your own destiny.

Chapter 1:

What is the Mind?

If you are going to train your mind, you need to first truly understand what it is. The mind is everything. Every action begins with a thought. In order to build strength and resilience, you therefore need to begin your training with the mind.

The Spartans knew this, and this is why Spartan education began extremely early in life. Sparta is a city located in the region of Laconia, which can be found at the southernmost tip of the Greek peninsula. Though still a populous city today, in ancient times, Sparta was one of the most powerful city states in the Mediterranean. Another name for this city was Lacedaemon, one that is often used in literary sources from the period (Jarus, 2017).

There were two wars in the ancient period called the Peloponnesian Wars, in which Sparta clashed in battle with its powerful rival in the region, Athens. It was at the end of the second Peloponnesian War, in 404 BCE, when Sparta defeated Athens and became the supreme military and political power in the region. At the height of its power, the city of Sparta had no walls. The people preferred to defend their city with men, not stone. However, Sparta's glory was relatively short lived. Within a few decades, Sparta was defeated by the rising power of Thebes in the Battle of Leuctra, and while it still remained a powerful presence in the region, it was never able to regain the might that it enjoyed at the beginning of the 3rd century BCE (Jarus, 2017).

Sparta's glory days may be long over, but the legendary strength and fearlessness of its warriors continue to be celebrated to this day, inspiring Hollywood movies like *300* and even the popular video game series *Halo*. Of course, the legends and the reality can sometimes be quite different. Though Sparta was a respected martial culture, they weren't renowned for their literary or historic works, and so many of the accounts we have of Spartan culture from the period were written by people who weren't actually Spartans themselves, further blurring the line between fact and fiction. To truly understand the Spartan mindset, we have to learn from the Spartans themselves (Jarus, 2017).

The first human settlement in the Spartan region dates back 3,500 years, though the city itself wouldn't be founded until the first millennium BCE. By the time the city was founded, its culture was already complex and advanced. In 2015, archaeologists uncovered a 10-room complex containing a number of ancient documents written in a language named "Linear B" by scientists. Beautiful murals were uncovered on the walls of the complex, and a number of bronze weapons were found in and around the site (Jarus, 2017).

Scientists can date this palace back to the 14th century BCE, at which point it was presumably destroyed by fire. The presence of this palace indicates that there may have been an older city that existed closer to the site of the city that would eventually become Sparta, but more archaeological evidence of such a city has yet to be uncovered. However, the presence of the palace and its contents indicates that there was already a thriving, advanced civilization in the region as far back as the 14th century BCE. New research suggests that Greece was suffering from a severe drought at the time that the palace burned down, which may perhaps explain the fire itself and the lack of archaeological evidence of the city it was part of (Jarus, 2017).

It wasn't until the early Iron Age (around 1000 BCE), that the four villages of Limnae, Pitana, Mesoa, and Cynosoura, would combine to form the city of Sparta. The early success of the city has just as much to do with its location as it does with the local culture, however. The Eurotas Valley in which Sparta is located is extremely fertile and provided the people of Sparta with an abundance of food and farmable land. The word "sparta" itself comes from an ancient Greek verb that means "to sow," a nod to the successful agricultural beginnings of the city (Jarus, 2017).

Perhaps ironically, early Spartans were not known for their military prowess, but for their artistic skills. The city was famous for its pottery, and Spartan vases have been unearthed as far away as Libya and Turkey. It was even known for its impressive ivory statues until about the 6th century BCE (Janus, 2017).

Spartan poetry was another artistic pursuit in which the early city was culturally dominant. In fact, there are more surviving literary documents and evidence of poetic activity from 7th century Sparta than from any other city-state in the region, including Athens and Thebes, who we tend to think of now as the "cultured" or "literary" cities of the Peloponnese. While much of this poetry only survives in fragments, mostly in recorded excerpts from local festivals, what it reveals is how the city's early artistic pursuits and cultured mentality began to be applied to the art of war (Janus, 2017).

But the main event that turned Sparta from a primarily artistic society to a military one was the city's conquest of Messenia, a region just to the west of Sparta. This conquest began in the 8th century BCE, and marks a change in Spartan culture and mindset. During the conquest, the people of Messenia were brought back to Sparta as slaves, beginning a crucial change in the way that Spartan society was structured. Because of the abundance of slave labor, Spartan adult males no longer had to worry about the performance of manual labor (Janus, 2017).

However, what they did have to worry about was control of all of these slaves. Historians from the period describe creations of what we might consider death squads and other relatively cruel methods of keeping slaves in line and preventing them from escaping. Spartan poetry from this time also starts to reflect a change in mindset, revealing that the culture was slowly beginning to transition from one primarily concerned with art and agriculture to one increasingly concerned with war and conquest (Janus, 2017).

With manual labor no longer necessary for the average Spartan citizen, more time and energy was available for military training. Over the years, the city developed a civilian training system that was meant to prepare its children for the harshness of war. But what is unique about the Spartan military philosophies is their emphasis on mindset and personal character. The deep preoccupations with mental discipline and the importance of perspective that came from the city's artistic past were preserved in the new martial systems, and this preoccupation with the mind is what would ultimately make Spartans the fiercest warriors of the time (Janus, 2017).

It was understood that mindset was critical to success, and therefore, Spartan education started extremely early. Boys were taken from their homes at age seven, to be raised in a barracks with boys all the way up to the age of 18. This education was notoriously harsh. Boys were whipped to instill them with respect and obedience, given little clothing to make them tough, and starved to make them resistant to hunger (Janus, 2017).

When they felt hungry, they were encouraged to steal food, but were punished severely if they were actually caught in the act. Slowly but surely, Spartan boys would grow and progress through this training system until the age of 20, when they would finally be allowed to join a communal mess (shared dining space) and be welcomed as an adult male citizen of Sparta. Every man in the mess was expected to contribute a certain amount of food to the community, and all were expected to continue training rigorously to maintain both their mental and physical discipline (Janus, 2017).

There was no room in this system for weakness or error. Those who could not fight due to disability were often mocked or cast out of society altogether, while those who fought *despite* obvious disability or handicaps were rewarded above all. Infants judged to have a disability at birth were often killed, as they were deemed to have no place in a society that valued both physical and mental perfection (Janus, 2017).

This harsh disciplinary world wasn't just for men, either. Though women were not expected to fight in a military capacity, they were expected to be in excellent physical shape, just as men were. Young women began training in athletics from an early age, and running, wrestling, discus and javelin throwing were all standard fixtures in a girl's education. They also learned how to ride and care for horses, and Spartan women were known for their ability to ride and fight on horseback (Janus, 2017).

This world may seem harsh and cruel, and in many ways it was. What we can take from this unbelievably harsh world, however, is the Spartan view of the mind. These practices seem barbaric to us now, but to Spartans, it was the height of culture and discipline. The mind, they knew, had to be made strong.

Focus, creativity, and resilience were skills, ones that needed constant practice in order to remain sharp. They looked at mental discipline and physical discipline as two sides of the same coin, understanding that physical training improved the mind, and that mental training improved the physical body. The harsh physical components of their training weren't meant to break people down. In fact, they ultimately did the opposite. The Spartans knew that if you believed yourself to be strong, you would be, and if you believed yourself to be weak, then you would be. They understood that your capabilities were only as good as your beliefs in yourself. Whatever you knew yourself to be capable of achieving, you would achieve. They intentionally put themselves into challenging situations in order to prove to themselves just how strong they were, and just how much they were able to achieve. This made them fierce warriors and superior athletes because, whenever they found themselves faced with real-world challenges, they had no doubt in their ability to overcome those obstacles. What's more, they understood that there was far more value in fighting valiantly and failing than running away from challenges without giving their all (N.G., 2020).

Beyond the Brain

These are the values that we can pull from the Spartan worldview to improve our own mental faculties in the modern day. Though they applied their beliefs in an extreme way, the Spartan mindset has parallels in other philosophies, including Buddhism and Stoicism.

Buddhists make a distinction between the "brain" and the "mind." The brain, in the Buddhist view, is yet another physical organ of the body, like the heart or the stomach. The mind, on the other hand, is something beyond the physical. Buddhists see the body and the mind as being and behaving distinctly from one another. For example, sometimes the body is relaxed, but the mind is active and wide awake. On the other hand, while we're engaged in intense physical activity, the mind may be relaxed while the body is active and charged with energy (Gyatso, n.d.).

Buddhist scriptures compare the physical body to a house, and the mind is compared to a guest living within the house. When we die, our mind or spirit leaves the body for somewhere else, just as a guest will eventually leave the house they are staying in. The mind, unlike the physical brain, is formless. Buddhists see the mind as an abstract continuum that helps us to perceive and understand the world around us (Gyatso, n.d.).

Like the Spartans, however, Buddhists recognize that states of mind can have a very real effect on how we interact with the world. What Buddhists call "disturbed" states of mind are feelings like anger, jealousy, and desirous attachment. These states contribute to suffering because they lead to delusions. They influence the way that we perceive the world around us. If we are filled with anger, for example, then we start to see anger and aggression reflected in the world around us. If we are jealous, we start to unfavorably compare ourselves with others (Gyatso, n.d.).

Suffering, says Buddhism, does not come from external factors like other people, material conditions, or the structures of society. Instead, it's caused by deluded states of mind. The essence of Buddhist meditations and spiritual practices is to overcome deluded states of mind and reach a state of inner peace. This state is the only state in which we can accurately see the world for what it really is, and experience the mind of mental focus and control we need to overcome challenges or difficulties (Gyatso, n.d.).

Liberation from suffering, therefore, cannot happen externally. The only way to become free of suffering is to liberate the mind. The Spartans may not have worded their philosophy this way, but their beliefs were ultimately very similar. They understood that a man is only as strong as he perceives himself to be, and their rigorous training was about proving to themselves how strong they really were. Instead of relying on meditations or positive language, they actively put themselves in harm's way. Every challenge that they successfully endured proved further to themselves and to others in their community that they were strong, powerful, and capable of overcoming all obstacles. Anyone who allowed external factors, including physical weakness or social pressures, to stop them from performing at their best was not respected because it ran contrary to this radical belief in the power of perception. If you allowed yourself to be limited by external factors, then you didn't have the mental resilience to overcome the challenges of war.

What the Spartan concept of the mind teaches us is that the mind is the foundation of our existence. Strength of any kind begins with the mind. You can't become physically strong if you don't have the mental discipline to train every day. You can't become intellectually strong if you don't have the mental discipline to study every day. You can't become emotionally strong if you don't have the mental discipline to view your emotions in a mindful and grounded way. In this way, the Spartans believed that all people had the ability to become strong. Strength for them wasn't something that you were born with. It had nothing to do with social status or genetics. It was a skill, something that had to be practiced every single day. Strength for them was a lifestyle, and a lifestyle must necessarily begin with a mindset.

The incredible feats of strength that Spartan warriors performed would never have been possible without the incredible mental discipline that these men and women had instilled in them from a very young age. They had no empathy for weakness, not because they were cruel or savage people, but because they radically believed that weakness was simply the product of laziness. Weakness was simply an indicator of poor mental discipline. Moments of weakness meant that you had to train even harder.

This is a major way in which the Spartan and Buddhist mindsets are very similar. Just as Buddhists believe that all suffering comes from within, Spartans believed that failure was simply the result of not getting enough practice. For example, let's look to the Spartan practice of encouraging young boys to steal food when they were hungry.

The boys were punished severely when they got caught stealing, even though stealing was their only option for survival. It seems harsh, even abusive (and perhaps it was), but the idea was to teach these young boys that if they wanted something, they had to go out and get it themselves. But, it also taught them that advocating for themselves wasn't always going to be rewarded by the world. There would always be social expectations, physical impairments, laws, and cruel people out there in the world ready to stop them from getting what they needed. It was an extreme lesson in self-reliance, and an extreme lesson in how not to depend on external circumstances for inner satisfaction. In other words, the lesson that these boys were being taught was: *If you need more food, find a way to get it. If you fail, accept your punishment and try again. Next time, you'll be a much better thief.*

Harsh physical training, for Spartan men and women, wasn't viewed as a form of punishment. It was about showing them that true suffering wasn't physical, but mental. Again, there's a distinct overlap with Buddhist philosophy here, which dictates that suffering is not a physical sensation but a state of mind. Spartans eventually learned to embrace physical challenges as something fun, something that they enjoyed because they knew that enduring and learning from physical pain would make them stronger in the end. Though failure was socially frowned upon, they learned not to fear it. They accepted the social punishment of failure, and learned from their mistakes so that next time they were in such a situation, they would be more likely to succeed. Spartans accepted failure, but they did not accept defeat. They understood that losing one battle (metaphorically and literally) had nothing to do with their ability to win the war.

This book isn't going to recommend living like a Spartan, nor is going to recommend starving or torturing yourself in order to harden yourself to pain. As you know by now, life will inevitably throw hardships at you without you having to create them for yourself. What you can learn from the Spartan philosophies, and what Spartan mental training looks like in today's world, is this radical sense of self-reliance.

You are the master of your own destiny. There are no external forces that can keep you down, no laws, social conditions, or financial realities that are too oppressive for you to overcome. If you want something from life, you *do* have the ability to go out and get it. In order to go out and get it, however, you have to be completely, totally confident in your ability to overcome the challenges in front of you. This is where strength training comes in. The stronger you are mentally, the more skill you'll have in overcoming mental and emotional challenges.

You would never hear a Spartan complaining about life not being fair, and you certainly would never hear a Spartan utter the words "I can't." Part of Spartan mental toughness is accepting that the world isn't fair. There are rules set up to keep you from succeeding, people who don't respect your right to be happy and successful, and social norms that put you at a disadvantage from the moment you were born. Accepting this reality doesn't mean shrugging your shoulders and saying to yourself, "Well, I guess this is the best I can do." It means understanding that the odds are stacked against you and winning the game anyway.

Remember, Spartans had a particularly cruel view of people with physical disabilities. But the people that they revered most were those who were seen to overcome their disability in order to fight with just as much strength and courage as those who were fully able-bodied. When we start incorporating Spartan mental toughness into our own mindset, it doesn't mean losing our sense of compassion or empathy for others. But it does mean that we have to stop looking at our weaknesses and limitations (whatever we perceive those to be) as reasons why we "can't" achieve the things that we want to achieve. The Spartans looked at their own limitations as things that would make victory more difficult, not as things that would make victory impossible.

Stoicism and the Spartan Mindset

Stoicism is a philosophy that was born in Ancient Rome, but it, too, contains echoes of the Spartan ideas that our minds are far more than our brains, and that our perception of our own abilities has everything to do with our ability to achieve success. The Stoics weren't warriors, they were philosophers, and their ideas continue to be celebrated today. In particular, the Stoic philosophy of mind is something that continues to be relevant. The Stoic philosophy of mind is one of the most advanced and complex in the entire classical world. Unlike Buddhists, the Stoics actually rejected the idea that the mind was incorporeal. Instead, they argued that the mind, or the spirit, had a physical component and had roots in the real world. They believed that all mental states were products of the "corporeal," or physical, soul, and that all of a person's actions were therefore a direct result of the conditions of the mind (Rubarth, n.d.).

In the Stoic mindset, the "mind" and the "soul" were essentially the same thing, and this soul took the form of a fiery, physical breath within the body. They believed that the soul pervaded the entire body and was a highly sensitive energy that brought information about the physical world back to the central, commanding center of the soul located in the chest. Once there, information about the world was processed and experienced. For the Stoics, as for the Spartans, mind and body were one and the same. Thought, language, and behavior were all intimately connected in both philosophies. The Stoics believed that mental content and behaviors were the direct result of perception, and that altering one's perception was the secret to altering both one's internal experiences (thoughts, feelings, attitudes, beliefs) as well as altering one's actions, behaviors, and speech. Like the Spartan martial philosophies, the Stoic philosophy of mind was also a philosophy of action (Rubarth, n.d.).

The Stoics famously rejected the ideas of the Greek philosophers Plato and Aristotle, who both maintained that the mind/soul had both rational and irrational properties. Instead, the Stoics argued that everything that happens in the mind is rational. They held that "passions," flaws, or weaknesses weren't the result of inherent irrational properties, but were simply the result of errors in judgment. In other words, the way that we feel about ourselves and our place in the world has everything to do with the way that we're processing information from the outside. If we perceive the world to be a dark and dangerous place, for example, then according to the Stoics, it would be perfectly rational for us to feel and behave in fearful or aggressive ways. Resolving problematic fear or anger responses, then, would have to begin with a change in perspective (Rubarth, n.d.).

The Greeks and Romans didn't see philosophy of mind as distinct from other forms of philosophy. Perception, imagination, thought, intelligence, emotion, memory, identity, and behavior are all things that we think of as belonging to the realm of psychology and cognitive science today. But for the Greeks and Romans, these things were just as much the territory of the soul as they were of the psyche. These things had just as much to do with spirituality, lifestyle, and worldview as they did with the way the brain works. As such, both the Stoics and the Spartans understood that mental and emotional strength were things one was born with. They were something one had to learn, practice, and study (Rubarth, n.d.).

The Spartan mindset can sometimes be difficult for contemporary people to understand because the Ancient Greek concept of the mind was very different from how we understand the mind today. In the contemporary world, we often make a sharp distinction between mind and body. When we think of the "mind," we typically think of cognitive abilities and possibly our sense of identity.

The Greek concept of mind, however, was not exclusive from the body. They understood the mind to be the essence of life, the spark that gives the physical body animation and energy. For them, the mind wasn't just about thinking, perceiving, imagining, and reasoning. The mind was also the force behind bodily processes like respiration, digestion, procreation, growth, and physical motion. This link between mind and body was particularly strong in Spartan thinking. Long after the glory days of Sparta, the Roman Stoics continued and expanded on this idea that the functions of mind and body are deeply intertwined (Rubarth, n.d.).

Modern psychology is slowly starting to appreciate the truths in the Stoic and Spartan way of thinking. Only recently are studies beginning to demonstrate how the mind (not just the brain) and the body are more connected than we once supposed. It's now fairly commonly accepted that "mental" states like depression and anxiety can have very real, physical effects on the body and its functions. Studies of PTSD have demonstrated that trauma, even mental or emotional trauma, can physically change the body's chemistry and the brain's basic functions. We don't just feel like we have more energy and strength when we're in a relaxed or confident state of mind; we *are* stronger and more energetic.

The Stoics, though they perceived mind and body to be closely interconnected, divided their philosophy into three main parts: logic, ethics, and physics. Teachings regarding the mind/soul, however, could be found in all three parts. In physics, the Stoics emphasized the physical aspects of the soul, and its role in the functioning of the human body. In logic, the Stoics theorized that there was no objective "meaning" or "truth," but that these concepts were related to thoughts, perceptions, and other psychological processes within the individual person. From this, the Stoics developed a sophisticated philosophy of mental content and intentionality, one that has very strong echoes with the Spartan philosophies of mental strength translating to physical strength. Finally, the Stoics argued in ethics that morality, again, was not objective, but based in emotions and emotionally-based actions. The development of one's cognitive faculties, therefore, was intimately connected to one's ethics. One's psychology was the central core of their being. The mind was (quite literally) what defined an individual's physical and emotional reality, and therefore was the root of all actions, attitudes, beliefs, and behaviors (Rubarth, n.d.).

Zeno of Citium (335-263BCE) was the founder of Stoicism. He and his student Cleanthes (331-232BCE) began writing and speaking about the mind as a physical presence within the body, often described as a kind of heat or inner fire. However, it was the teachings of the philosopher Chrysippus (280-207BCE) that would ultimately make Stoicism what it is today. It was Chrysippus who first proposed that the human soul was like a hot breath or wind that permeated the body. Different cognitive functions, according to Chrysippus, could also be attributed to activities of the soul. This vital soul substance that animated humans was believed to be present in all things, a kind of world-soul that animated all life on earth. This "world-soul" would come to be identified by the Stoics with Zeus, the supreme god of the Olympians in Ancient Greek mythic tradition. Deviating from the traditional anthropomorphic view of the gods, however, the Stoics believed Zeus to be a kind of fiery energy, one that enables all life to grow and create. In other words, the Stoics viewed the world to be a living organism, rather than a dead lump of rock (Rubarth, n.d.).

This interplay between the physical and the mental/spiritual is critical to understanding Stoic philosophy, and it's not that far removed from the Spartan worldview. The Stoic philosophy was more complicated and a bit more mystical, identifying the soul as a mixture of the elements air and fire and spending a great deal of time contemplating different possible physical manifestations of the soul within the body. But the Stoics also believed that the same soul energy, the same force behind the human mind, was the force that created and sustained all life on earth. The human mind, therefore, was the presence of the divine, endowing human beings with reason and intelligence (Rubarth, n.d.).

The Stoics argued firmly that the mind/soul was a physical, bodily substance, not a separate entity the way that Buddhists understand it. However, this doesn't mean that the Stoics didn't believe in the existence of a soul, or that our thoughts were merely the products of physical signaling in the brain, the way that cognitive psychologists do today. The Stoics, like Buddhists, believed that there was a difference between mind/soul and physical matter. They believed that the mind and body were inextricably connected, but this doesn't mean that they believed the mind was something that could be physically seen or touched in the body like an organ.

Instead, they believed that matter and spirit were just two sides of the same coin, two manifestations of the same energy. They saw the mental or spiritual as active existence, and they saw physical matter as passive. Matter is cold, still, and physical. It gets its motion, animation, and vitality from spirit. Similar to Buddhist philosophies, then, the Stoics believed that, though mind and body could behave in distinct and different ways, the two were intrinsically connected to one another. Certain substances could be stronger in one kind of energy or the other, but humans, they believed, had a healthy mix of both (Rubarth, n.d.).

This might seem like heady, heavy stuff, but the Spartans didn't spend as much time as the Stoics pondering over abstract theology. They grasped the essence of the philosophy, which is that the mind is much more than the physical brain, but it's also rooted in our physical bodies and physical experiences. The Spartans understood that by training their physical bodies to be strong, they were also training their minds to be strong and vice versa.

What we can take from this in the modern world is that our mindset is just as important as our physical realities or our tangible skills. Whatever challenge you're facing, whether it's making enough money to pay your rent, constantly fighting with your romantic partner, or failing to find success in a job or field that you truly love, you *do* have the skills to overcome it.

The Spartan mindset isn't about "mind over matter." They literally believed that mind *is* matter. What you believe is possible is what's possible. If you accept external limitations, then you will be limited. To begin training your mind, and to learn true mental strength, you have to prove to yourself that you're strong enough to overcome any challenge that you set your mind to. Starving and whipping yourself aren't exactly viable or recommendable strategies today, but there are some practical exercises you can use to train your mind and body to be just as strong in the modern world as the Spartans once were on the ancient battlefields of Greece.

Chapter 2:

Why Do We Resist Our Discomforts?

Before you find any real ability to change yourself, you have to first understand yourself. Really understand yourself. While we're often very good at finding and celebrating our strengths, talents, and interests, we have a much more difficult time taking responsibility for our feelings and behaviors in times of discomfort, change, and fear. We often look at these moments as "dark" or "bad" times, and when we experience them, we tend to look critically at ourselves and our lives. If we're uncomfortable, we tend to think there's something wrong.

But the Spartans understood that discomfort is not only an inevitable part of life, but a very healthy and necessary part. Over the years, what the Spartans understood on a spiritual level has been validated by scientific, evolutionary, and psychological study today—that discomfort is a healthy and natural part of the human experience. It's something that helps us to grow and makes us stronger. More importantly, it's *necessary* for us to grow and become strong. Growth is uncomfortable, and that's ok.

It's true that fear and instability can lead to resistance, suffering, and unhappiness, but it doesn't have to be this way. Fear and discomfort don't have to be negative things, nor do they have to be indicators that there's something wrong with the way you live your life. Viewing our discomforts from a Spartan perspective means looking at moments of discomfort as opportunities. When you're feeling uncomfortable, it means that you're growing. This is a moment that, if approached correctly, can catapult you forward toward your goals. In the Spartan mindset, fear is your best friend. It's the thing that empowers you to make the changes that you need to make to become the most powerful version of yourself.

Think about your own discomforts. Now think about the way that you respond when you're in those kinds of situations or feeling those uncomfortable feelings. If you're like most people today, you probably spend a great deal of time avoiding being uncomfortable. This avoidance of discomfort limits your actions. It presents a mental or emotional barrier. Whenever you start to feel uncomfortable, you probably stop doing whatever you're doing. But does this avoidance of discomfort actually serve you in the long run?

If discomfort is a natural part of life, then why do you typically try to run away from it? The first step in developing mental strength is to embrace discomfort. Stop running. Don't shy away from the situation when you start to feel uncomfortable. And most importantly, stop viewing uncomfortable feelings as an indicator that something is "wrong" with yourself or with your life.

Embracing discomfort, however, is much easier said than done. The reason most of us avoid discomfort at all costs is because all discomfort is rooted in fear. When we feel negative feelings within ourselves, our natural reaction is to blame and project those negative feelings on the outside world. It's always someone else's fault, right? Whether you're feeling angry, frustrated, jealous, anxious, tired, or anything else unpleasant, your first reaction is to looking for something or someone around you to blame. It's your parents, your roommates, your job, the government, your nation, your education, or even the bad weather that's to blame for your unpleasant feelings. It's never the simple fact that you feel afraid.

Admitting that we feel fear is extremely difficult because it means admitting that we aren't in complete control over our lives. Admitting to fear means admitting to insecurity. It means coming to terms with the fact that there is something triggering us or making us feel incapable of caring for ourselves in some way. If you feel resistant to the idea that almost every negative experience in your life is rooted in fear, then you're hardly alone. But there are many fears that are extremely common to the human experience, and there are a few common (but destructive) behaviors or attitudes that humans adopt to help them cope with these fears.

Fear of the Uncertain

Cognitive science tells us that our brains are wired to resolve unknowns. When our brains are faced with uncertainty, the natural impulse is to create certainty. All of us are driven by an intense, emotional need to resolve unknowns immediately, and so our brains typically default to the easiest, fastest, and least-painful solution to every problem encountered. This is a great survival mechanism when we're faced with immediate, life-threatening problems. But most of the time, we tend to choose the easiest, rather than the best, option when faced with a problem. If we don't force ourselves to make choices or face truths that are long and difficult, then we never leave our comfort zones (Razzetti, 2019).

The reality, however, is that anticipation of change almost always causes more damage than the change itself. In order to embrace change, we have to find a way to become open to uncertainty. The only way to embrace the unknown is to take things one step at a time. Look at what's actually in front of you. Fight your fears and predictions of what is going to happen, and stop fighting reality (Razzetti, 2019).

Fear of Failure

No one wants to fail. This is especially true in a society where failure is often condemned and punished. But making mistakes is not only normal and inevitable, it's a necessary part of the learning process. You can't experiment or try new things if you're terrified of making a mistake. And if you stop experimenting, then you stop growing.

Perhaps Oscar Wilde says it best: experience is the name we give to our mistakes. This is a fear that also tends to compound on itself. The more afraid you are of making a mistake, the more likely you are to find flaws in yourself. Mistakes are inevitable. They are a healthy and normal part of the human experience. Accept the fact that you are vulnerable, and accept the fact that making mistakes doesn't make you wrong, bad, or defective in any way. On the contrary, it's perfection that's unnatural. Start thinking of mistakes as opportunities to learn and reflect, rather than indicators that there's something inherently wrong with you. Rather than resisting or even denying them, whenever you make a mistake, ask yourself what you can learn from the situation (Razzetti, 2019).

Fear of Being Ridiculed

We all want to look good in front of other people, especially people who we love and respect. This is what sometimes prompts us to hide or conceal things about ourselves. We unconsciously present ourselves to others in a way that we believe will make them appreciate and accept us. Sometimes this is healthy, but if you become consumed by the need to be liked by other people, then you start repressing your true, authentic self.

True emotional freedom happens when you stop caring about other people's opinions. FEAR is a popular psychological acronym that stands for False Evidence Appearing Real. It's true that people may laugh at you if you take risks, but how do you know that they won't laugh at you if you never take risks? How many opportunities have you let pass you by because you were afraid of what other people might think of you? No one masters something the first time they try it. Feeling and being awkward is always the first step in the learning process (Razzetti, 2019).

Fear of Losing Control

Remember, our brains are wired to find answers and solve problems. This is true even if we have no idea what's going on or what to do about it. It's this need for answers that often stops us from surrendering to the natural currents of life.

Fear of losing control is the root of the fear of change. When change happens, we are in the realm of the unknown, and that means that we are no longer in the driver's seat. We are no longer in control when we face something new. And feeling like you have no control is one of the scariest experiences you can have. In fact, there's a great deal of research linking unhappiness, helplessness, hopelessness, and depression with experiencing a loss of control. But the reality is that life is *always* out of your control. The only way to embrace a loss of control is to look only at what's right in front of you, and wait for the outcome to unfold (Razzetti, 2019).

Fear of Inadequacy

How many times a day do you tell yourself that you're not good enough? Every human feels inadequate or incapable at one point or another. However, feelings of inadequacy are rarely based in reality. When you find yourself feeling unworthy, it's often because you're either holding yourself to impossibly high standards, or comparing yourself to someone else. The grass always *seems* greener on the other side, but in reality, the grass is greener on the side that gets the most rain. But whenever we are faced with a challenge, we immediately begin to doubt our ability to successfully overcome it.

While it's sometimes healthy to pause and think before acting, hesitating too much can cause you to become trapped in your fears and prevent you from acting at all. Embracing change requires taking a leap into the unknown. Self-doubt is often touted as a sign of rationality, but the truth is actually the opposite. Self-doubt actually erodes your clarity, and inhibits your ability to look objectively at the situation. Self-doubt is yet another form of anticipating the outcome. Trust your gut, trust yourself, and just do it.

Fear of inadequacy is a bit of a paradox. Often, we aren't afraid that we're incapable, we're afraid to find out that we *are* capable. With great power comes great responsibility. It's often easier to shy away from challenges under the pretext that we just aren't strong enough or skilled enough to handle them. Being adequate and being good enough means taking on life's challenges, and that is definitely an uncomfortable role to be in.

How to Embrace Change

Fear is what ultimately causes us to resist change, and as long as we are engaged in resistance, we are incapable of being productive. This, ultimately, is what causes suffering. This is what causes us to feel stuck, out of control, and held back. We find ourselves incapable of moving forward, but what we don't understand is that it's our own resistance that's preventing our growth. Growth may be uncomfortable or even painful, but suffering comes from a lack of growth. Suffering is what happens when we cease to grow and cease to change.

Suffering manifests in all kinds of unpleasant ways, including addiction, depression, and anger. But we allow it into our lives because we are afraid of what might happen if we let go and embrace the unknown. We are afraid of change because we tend to obsess over what we stand to lose, rather than looking forward to the things we have to gain. But change is inevitable. Perhaps ironically, change is the *only* thing in life that's certain, and so to fear it is ultimately a bit silly. Things are changing every moment of every day. What we often don't realize is that avoiding the change still changes the situation. When faced with an unknown, your only choice is to embrace it. Avoiding it won't preserve anything, nor will it give you more control over the outcome.

But embracing change is uncomfortable, and so it is much easier said than done. However, when we start avoiding change *because* it's uncomfortable, we start allowing today's discomfort to impact our future successes. The most difficult part of achieving your goals is pushing through the discomfort that inevitably comes with change. This is where a lot of people give up. The moment they start to experience some really challenging feelings, they decide that the amount of discomfort they're feeling is an indicator that whatever they're striving for just "wasn't meant to be." But uncomfortable feelings are part of the processes, as is the temptation to give up on your dreams. If you quit your job to pursue your passions, for example, then in six months when you find yourself selling your car in order to pay your rent, the security of an office job will seem really appealing. If you really want a master's degree and get rejected from all of the programs you applied to, you're going to find it difficult to send out another batch of applications in the spring. If you truly love someone but fear getting hurt by them, you will probably feel extremely distressed when the first sign of conflict appears. In all of these situations and more, it's all too common to take the uncomfortable feelings or situations as a sign that you're barking up the wrong tree. But selling your car to pay your rent or getting rejected from your desired master's programs *aren't* signs of failure. Instead, they're signs that you still have something to learn before you can achieve your desired goal. If you give up, then you're guaranteeing that you'll never get what you want from life.

Being mentally strong doesn't mean that you never hear that little inner voice telling you to go back and give up. Mental resilience means hearing the inner voice that tells you it's "too hard" or "not worth it" to achieve your goals and ignoring it. If you truly want something, then it *is* worth it to keep striving for it. Think of the Spartan boys who had to steal food to survive. Their options were this: find a way to succeed, or starve. Your goal may not be as visceral as stealing food to survive, but you should view it in the same terms. If you want something, then giving up shouldn't even be entertained as an option. Sometimes we do find our goals, wants, or needs changing, but even if that does happen, you'll never regret the lessons you've learned or the skills you've attained in the process of fighting to achieve your goals or live your passions. What we *do* find ourselves regretting are the opportunities we talked ourselves out of taking because we were too afraid to do what needed to be done to achieve our dreams. Fortunately, there are a few demonstrated tactics that you can use to help yourself become more comfortable with change and discomfort when it inevitably rears its ugly head (Deschene, 2015).

Identify Potential Challenges and Decide That You Can Meet Them

Whenever you find yourself faced with a challenge, take a moment to mentally step back. List all of the factors that might encourage you to quit. Be as specific as possible. What sacrifices are you being asked to make, and which will be the most difficult for you? What changes are you facing, and which will push you furthest outside of your comfort zone?

Once you've thought about these questions, however, the next thing to ask yourself is what you stand to gain from pushing forward. Only then can you accurately judge if the discomfort you're experiencing now will be worth the reward in the future.

Observe Your Emotions Without Resisting Them

Rushes of emotion are a natural and inevitable part of being human. We become obsessed with "controlling" our emotions or thoughts when we start to make them part of our identity. But you are not your feelings, and you are not your thoughts. Your existence is far more complicated than the inner workings of your mind.

If you stop resisting your feelings, then you'll find yourself able to experience life without analyzing, judging, forming opinions, reliving the past, or worrying about the future. Allow yourself to notice your feelings. Allow yourself to feel your feelings. Whenever a feeling comes up, remember that it's not permanent. Negative feelings like fear, anxiety, or paranoia are uncomfortable, but they won't last forever. Allowing yourself to feel these uncomfortable feelings is the only way to stop them from controlling your thoughts and behaviors. When you stop resisting your feelings, you'll find it much easier to let them go (Deschene, 2015).

When Your Emotions Get Louder, Challenge Them With More Emotions

All of us have a constant inner monologue of thoughts, feelings, plans, and attitudes. But in order to fully experience and accept the present moment, we need to find a healthy way to quiet that inner monologue.

The truth is that, no matter how mentally resilient you are, you'll always be bouncing back and forth between observing your mind and submitting to it. That's only natural, and that's why so many mentally strong people have developed strategies for overcoming the moments when their emotions feel particularly powerful.

One strategy is to create an inner dialogue with your future self. Whenever you find yourself feeling scared and wanting to give into that fear, think about yourself a week from now. Will your future self look back on your actions with pride and satisfaction? Don't allow this to become a moment that you'll regret. No matter how uncomfortable change may be, your actions today set up your feelings tomorrow. Whenever you check in with your future self, you'll always find that moving through your fear is worth it.

Celebrate All Your Minor Victories

When you have large goals, it's easy to feel dissatisfied until they have been fully achieved. If your life's passion is to produce a feature film, for example, you probably won't celebrate securing the first location as a major victory.

But it is. Every victory is a victory. Our accomplishments only seem small when we compare them with future achievements that we're still working toward. But every single accomplishment is a testament to how talented, capable, driven, and powerful you truly are. If you don't give yourself that credit, then you'll eventually find yourself becoming more and more discouraged.

Call Yourself a Liar

People give up on their dreams because they stop believing that the life they want to live is possible for them. How many times have you stopped yourself from taking action because you're not being "realistic" or because you've somehow rationalized that the things you want aren't possible in "real" life? Sometimes, we even trick ourselves into thinking we don't really want the things that we want. It's easier to give up than to live constantly dissatisfied.

How often have you found yourself saying things like, "I didn't want that promotion anyway," or "Thankfully

I didn't get that job - it would have been far too much travel." Sometimes this is true. We often pursue things that look good, only to find that the reality is not what we had imagined it to be. However, often we look at the flaws or potential discomforts that come with achieving our goals in order to give ourselves permission to quit. Don't allow yourself to do this. Whenever you find yourself rationalizing your way out of getting something that you want, remind yourself that you *can* do this, that you *do* want it, and that you will therefore keep trying to get it.

This is your chance to live the life you want to live. The opportunity for change is right now. The connection you've been hoping to make is you. The inspiration you've been looking for is you. Stop waiting for someone else to come and give you what you want. Achieving your goals necessitates being bold. Being brave means feeling afraid and taking action anyway. Stop resisting change, and instead embrace it as an opportunity to acquire new strength, new skills, and new accomplishments.

How to Embrace Fear

However, fear isn't always an act of self-sabotage. Anxiety is something that all humans experience from time to time. Embracing fear isn't about making it go away or pushing it aside in order to overcome a certain obstacle. Embracing fear is about using your fear to help you achieve your goals. Fear and anxiety help to increase our attention span and motivate us to put forth a little extra effort to overcome the challenges in front of us. Even anticipatory fear can be your friend, enhancing your experience of a situation by making it more exciting or exhilarating.

The trick is to not let fear overwhelm your ability to function. The true difference between success and failure is not turning off or ignoring your fear, but being able to understand the difference between helpful and harmful fear. Anxiety is simply an intense feeling of fear, and when it appears, it's simply giving us information about the world around us. No fear is invalid or illegitimate. The skill of using and embracing fear is understanding where the fear is coming from. Are you feeling anxiety because you've stepped outside of your comfort zone? Or are you feeling anxiety because something truly dangerous is in front of you?

For example, if you're someone who prefers to stay at home on the weekends, it's natural to feel a bit of fear and discomfort when you go out to a party or a bar. This doesn't necessarily mean that parties are "bad" or "dangerous." It just means that you're doing something new that you aren't used to or fully comfortable with.

In the example of the party, if you're going out more because you want to make more friends or meet a romantic partner, then the expert advice would most likely be to push through your discomfort in order to achieve your goals. If you act in spite of your fear, then you will eventually become comfortable at parties or bars and your social skills will grow as a result. The only problem with that approach is this: what happens if you *don't* achieve your goal? If you go to the party and you have a really good time, then you'll feel empowered to be more social and go out more often. But if you don't, the opposite is likely to happen. If you go to the party and spend the entire night standing awkwardly alone by the punch bowl, you're going to feel absolutely miserable when you get home. Pushing yourself outside of the comfort zone and failing can make it much more difficult to take risks and push yourself again in the future.

The crucial difference is the difference between discomfort and distress. Discomfort is unpleasant, but ultimately, it's tolerable. When you feel discomfort, imagining doing what you want to do will still feel exciting and rewarding. This is the type of fear to push through, as it's often related to the common fears of change and failure. Distress, however, is the kind of fear that actively limits your ability to perform, and therefore can prevent you from achieving your goals. For example, if you dream of becoming a famous musician, but your anxiety causes you to freeze up every time you're on stage, then what you're experiencing is distress, not discomfort. Distress actively stops you from achieving your goals, even if you choose to act in spite of it. When you are experiencing distress, this is not the right time to act. Acting in the face of discomfort ultimately leads to success, but forcing yourself to act in the face of distress is setting yourself up for failure.

Distress happens when we step a little too far outside of our comfort zone. When experiencing distress, take a mental step back. Try to refocus on the reasons why you wanted to take this major step in the first place. If you still feel that the danger you're putting yourself in is worth the potential rewards, then you can go ahead and take the risks you need to take to learn and grow. But if you find yourself paralyzed with fear, it may be worth it to break your big goals down into smaller, more manageable chunks. Give yourself small challenges that only cause you a bit of discomfort, rather than forcing yourself to take a big leap that causes distress and failure. Remember that discomfort ultimately feels more good than bad, while distress ultimately feels more bad than good (Vilhauer, 2018).

Embracing fear means putting a certain amount of trust in yourself. If you're constantly fighting to stay in your comfort zone, then you're doing yourself just as much damage as you would if you took a big risk. In the long run, you may even be doing more damage, because no matter how catastrophic your failure may be, there's always a lesson to be learned from trying something new. Fear, failure, and discomfort are all unpleasant and painful feelings, but none of them cause suffering. True suffering happens when we cease to grow.

This can take many different forms, depending on who the person is, what their life goals are, and what kinds of traumas or negative experiences they've had in the past. Past failures can be paralyzing, teaching us to fear the same situation when it arises again.

What mindfulness and other spiritual practices teach us is that overcoming fear is not something you can do with other people. Embracing fear is something that can only be done alone. No matter how much comfort or encouragement we get from others, the truth is that it's often external events that rock our sense of safety and security. This is why it's so easy to blame negative and intense emotions on external forces. When negative feelings do arise, we often assume that to be strong and resilient means to toss these negative feelings aside and never confront them.

But the truth is the opposite. Embracing your fear means allowing yourself to experience it, and understanding that no feeling is permanent or invalid. Fear is simply the way that we respond to the difficult or painful moments that lead to our growth. Fear is an indicator that we have something still to learn. Things are always changing, but we only experience fear when we encounter a change that threatens our sense of security.

Learning to embrace fear means learning to have a great deal of patience with yourself. But if you resist pain, you'll find that your very resistance causes you even more suffering, difficulty, and unhappiness than simply feeling that pain when it arises. Your darkest moment doesn't have to define your entire existence. One moment of pain might feel like the end of the world, but if you push through, then that pain will eventually recede. Better still, you'll come out on the other side of that pain a stronger, wiser person.

Striving, longing, and expecting are three of the major ways that our minds cope with fear. Letting go of fixed outcomes is the most powerful way to become comfortable with change, and to embrace the fear or anxiety that all change initiates within us. The only real, permanent solution to any problem is to accept that the problem exists and bend your mind toward solving it. Resisting reality by placing expectations or engaging in wishful thinking will only make you deeply unhappy and stop you from taking any real action to get what you need or let go of things that aren't serving you.

Embracing fear, then, means accepting the reality of what's right in front of you. When pain emerges, resist the urge to run from it and just experience it. The Spartans understood the value of this lesson, and this is why they inflicted as much pain on themselves and their young ones as they could from a very early age. It seems unimaginably cruel, and in some ways it was, but it taught young Spartan boys that there was no escape from pain. It taught them the immeasurably valuable lesson that the only way to truly cope with pain is to accept it. Accepting pain means trusting that you have what it takes to survive it. Trust that the pain you're experiencing now isn't going to kill you, or irreparably damage you.

To embrace your fears, you must fully commit to honoring yourself and your needs. We do a great deal of mental gymnastics sometimes in order to convince ourselves that we don't really want what we want, or that we don't really need what we need. We do those mental gymnastics to avoid having to go through the necessary difficulties that will arise when we choose to fight for those things. When we fail, make mistakes, or encounter difficulties, we choose to blame the outside world for our failures. If another person or situation is holding us back, then there's "nothing" we can do, and that means we don't have to keep trying. It's much easier to wallow in comfortable misery than it is to work through beneficial pain.

Stop allowing yourself to take the easy way out. Let go of fears, future projections, and imaginary worries.

Most importantly, let go of the idea that success means protecting yourself from experiencing pain. More often than not, the pain we think we're going to experience based on past conditioning is far worse than the pain we actually experience when we find ourselves in the thick of a difficult situation. Allowing yourself to experience your fear is acknowledging the existence of that conditioning. Allowing yourself to work with your fear, rather than against it, means that you're learning a new lesson, and it also means being aware that you're creating new mental conditions for yourself to take to future challenges (Niederhofer, 2017).

Comfort is often held up by our society as an indicator of happiness and success. But as any addict can tell you, pleasure doesn't always lead to happiness. And as any Spartan could have told you, pain doesn't necessarily lead to unhappiness. Embracing fear doesn't necessarily mean intentionally putting yourself in dangerous or painful situations. It means accepting the fact that life is inevitably going to put us in undesirable circumstances. If we can declare to ourselves the intention to push through painful events, then our minds can immediately focus on overcoming the pain in front of us, rather than engaging in coping mechanisms to shield ourselves from the reality of that pain. Resistance, escapism, and denial will only serve to intensify the pain (Barbauta, n.d.).

This is why embracing fear, change, and discomfort all go hand in hand. Change is often uncomfortable or painful, initiating feelings of fear as we anticipate the negative consequences of facing the situation in front of us. Embracing fear means embracing reality.

Running from fear or trying to insulate yourself from it will inevitably result in you running away from reality, and ultimately running away from your true self. Disasters and trying times happen to everyone. Some people appear to have it "easier" than others because some people approach negative situations with resilience, while others allow the negative circumstances of their life to overwhelm and limit them (Fahkry, 2018).

Chapter 3:

The North Star and What Spartans Knew That We've Forgotten

At this point, your mind is already transitioning into a more powerful stance. Having a north star or a "why" to guide you through life is perhaps the single most powerful thing you can do to build focus and resilience within yourself. Once you've found your "why," you can use it to build a decision-making framework against which you can weigh every decision you'll ever have to make, keeping you focused, calm, and brave in the face of any challenge and therefore bringing you to previously unimagined heights of success.

Most of us are familiar with the nautical concept of the north star. Astronomically speaking, it's the star Polaris, and its fixed position in the night sky has helped sailors across the globe to navigate on the open seas. A personal north star serves the same purpose, guiding you through life the way that Polaris guides sailors at night. A personal north star, essentially, is a life purpose. Without one, it's easy to feel lost and disoriented. With one, however, you'll be nearly unstoppable when it comes to achieving your goals (Ho, 2019).

The concept of a personal north star comes to us from the Spartans. Though their concept was much more community-oriented than individual, the concept can still be used by us today to help us achieve our personal goals. The north star exercise is something that set the Spartans apart from other warriors of their time, and helped to strengthen their minds in ways that other warriors were never able to achieve.

Finding your own purpose means finding something worth pursuing that defines your role in and contribution to the world. Whether your life's purpose is to be a great athlete, musician, father, surgeon, or romantic partner doesn't matter. The point is to find something that's worth devoting all of your mental, physical, and creative faculties to. Understanding your life's purpose gives you passion, energy, and determination. It gives you something to work toward, a personal north star to guide you when you face difficult choices or changes in your life (Ho, 2019).

The next step for you in your journey toward mental toughness is to find your own personal north star. Have you discovered your life's purpose? Are the majority of your energies focused on becoming the best person you can be?

Sometimes following your north star isn't easy. But the Spartans understood the value of pain as a teacher and motivator, to the point that they actively pursued it in order to make both their body and mind stronger.

Though all warriors have to come to some level of pain tolerance, the Spartans are still unique to this day for their willingness to intentionally put themselves in painful situations with the intention of becoming stronger. Theirs was the only training program that combined both physical and psychological strength training, such as starving the boys, encouraging them to steal, and then punishing them when caught.

Eventually, every Spartan would find their "north star," or the goal of becoming the greatest warrior they could possibly be. This goal gave them their life's purpose, and every single action they took throughout their lives was taken in the pursuit of this goal. This made difficult decisions much easier to make, because all they had to do was "look" to their north star for guidance. "If I do this, will it serve the purpose of becoming a better warrior?" If the answer was yes, then the decision was made, no matter how difficult or painful the action in front of them may have been.

This is why having a purpose is so crucial to achieving greatness. Without purpose, you won't have the motivation that you need to push through the really difficult moments or make the really difficult choices. Successful people know exactly what they want, and every choice they make in life is calculated to bring them just a bit closer to getting it. If you're struggling to achieve the things that you want or even find yourself constantly dissatisfied with your life, then it may be time for you to find your own north star.

Like the Spartans fighting for martial excellence, your north star will be the thing around which your entire life is ordered. And like the Spartans, once you find your life's purpose, you'll have an almost super-human ability to overcome any obstacles that stand in the way of you achieving that purpose. Once you've become fixated on a goal, then small things will no longer be able to hold you back from getting it. The only challenges that will even pose a threat to you will be big ones.

For example, imagine that you've decided to learn the electric guitar. You purchase all the equipment you need and subscribe to online guitar lessons. For the first few weeks, it's fun, it's enjoyable, and you can see yourself making progress. But then, one day, you accidentally snap the top string of the guitar while playing. For a casual learner, the hassle of purchasing a new string and learning how to restring a guitar might be enough to end the hobby altogether. But if your north star is to become a great musician, then you won't even think of letting this small bump in the road stop you from playing. Instead, you'll head straight to the nearest guitar shop, follow a YouTube tutorial that will teach you how to restring your guitar, and you'll be ready to go for next week's class.

Now, the next time you break a string, the process of restringing won't even seem like an obstacle. Rather, it will have just become a routine part of being a guitar player.

This focus and sense of purpose is what made the Spartans some of the most disciplined warriors on the planet, which is another reason why they were so tough. They never stopped training, from age seven until death. There was no "graduation" from a Spartan education, because the Spartans understood that a person never really stops growing. They feared no challenge because they had such a strong sense of purpose to guide them through difficult, dangerous, and fearsome situations. Ultimately, they knew that no matter how unpleasant the situation before them was, it was worth fighting for.

Knowing that you have something worth fighting for makes a big difference in how much pain you're willing to tolerate. More often than not, we find ourselves losing motivation when we lose sight of why we're doing what we're doing in the first place. If you find yourself constantly missing deadlines or skipping projects at work, it's time to remind yourself why you're at that job in the first place. Is this a stepping-stone for you to get a promotion or a better job in the future? Is this job paying your rent or providing for your family? Keeping sight of your "why" will make arduous, boring, or painful tasks much easier because no matter what comes your way, you know that all the discomfort you're experiencing now will be worth it in the future.

Having a north star is the difference between living care-free and living disciplined. You can't be disciplined on occasion, and you can't rely on discipline to make your choices for you. But if you're completely care-free and having nothing to guide you through life, then you'll start to find yourself drifting, incapable of mustering the necessary grit that you need to push yourself forward to achieve what you want to achieve.

Your north star is a big, lifelong goal around which you can orient smaller, finite goals. For example, if your north star is to become a great teacher, then the decisions to do well in high school in order to get into a good college, study hard to pass your college exams, fight to get into a good student-teaching program, and then hunt for a good job once you're qualified, will all be easy to make. The decision to stay in and study while all of your high school friends are out partying is a difficult one to make, but if you have a north star to guide you, then in your mind, there is no choice at all.

Having a north star helps you to find a sense of direction in life as well. If you want to become a great athlete, for example, then you won't spend years of your life wondering what to do with yourself. When in doubt, you'll always find yourself at the gym, working hard to build your strength, or studying nutrition to make sure you're putting the right foods into your body to maintain the strength you've worked so hard for.

To complement this sense of personal duty, the Spartans also followed a code of honor to serve and fight for one another. An individual Spartan would never put his fellow warriors in danger or harm's way in order to serve his own purposes, and trusted the men around him to do the same for him. When they were out in the battlefield, then, their motivation was doubled. The pursuit of becoming the best warrior you could be was paired with the strong need to protect the men around them from harm.

Sometimes we face difficult decisions that don't directly benefit us, but that serve to respect, protect, or otherwise value the people in our lives that are important to us. So that job that you hate may not be worth pursuing for your own sake, but if your wife and children are depending on your income to pay rent, then the Spartan code of honor tells you to keep performing with excellence until you've found another job.

How To Find Your North Star

The Spartans understood that there's a difference between being smart and being wise. A smart person sets goals, charting their progress against ambitious plans and constantly living in the pursuit of greatness. But a wise person roots themselves in a purpose, aligning their goals and actions to the pursuit of that purpose. The north star is that life's purpose, and it's something that you'll expect to be pursuing for the rest of your life. Your north star isn't a "goal," in the sense that there's no finite moment at which it's been achieved. Like the true north star, it's not a destination in and of itself, but a guiding light that helps you to get wherever you want to go.

The idea of a guiding star can be found in a number of spiritual and cultural traditions, ancient Sparta being just one. Many life coaches and spiritual leaders today even use this concept to help people find their purpose in life. Bill George's concept of "true north" and the ancient Indian concept of "dhruv tara" are just a few variations of the north star concept in other contexts (Kaipa, 2014).

A contemporary example of the power of a north star at work is the story of Dr. Govindappa Venkataswamy, the ophthalmologist who started the Aravind Eye Care System in 1976. When he started this business, "Dr. V" had no business plan, no money, no resources, and had severely crippled fingers. Today, Aravind not only sees 2.7 million patients every year, but achieves the commendable goal of treating most of them for free. This success story is so powerful that it's been required reading for all Harvard Business School students for the past ten years (Kaipa, 2014).

What the Spartans understood is that we all have a choice in creating the life we desire. It's our judgments, choices, and actions that have the most powerful impact on whether or not we live the life we want to live. Unlike traditional models of goal-setting, the north star stops us from obsessing about the future and prompts us to focus on what we have to do in the present moment (Kaipa, 2014).

Your north star will help you to align all of your energy, emotions, and actions in the service of your true life's purpose, whatever that purpose may be. Following your north star might not always be easy, but the *choice* to follow it is simple. In order to be a leader, paradoxically, you have to learn how to be a follower. Becoming successful is first about learning how to follow your inner calling, and how to be of service to your life's vision even when it's difficult, painful, or contradictory to the life path that others want you to follow.

Dr. V would not have been able to achieve what he achieved without a north star to guide him. He didn't set out with the "goal" of starting a successful eye care facility; he set out with the life's purpose of ending unnecessary blindness. To do that, he reasoned, he must first find a way for all people to have access to appropriate, compassionate, and high-quality eye care.

To do *that,* he reasoned, he would have to begin by setting up his own eye clinic that followed the basic principles he would ultimately like to see all eye care facilities follow, and that's exactly what he did.

In 1976, he founded an 11-bed clinic that was run on three basic principles: turn no one away regardless of their ability to pay, give all patients the same quality of care, and don't depend on any outside sources for funding. Since 1976, his vision has blossomed into the huge, global eye care facility that it is today. It will continue to grow, because Dr. V's life's purpose wasn't to become a successful entrepreneur or run one of the world's largest eye care facilities. His life purpose was to end unnecessary blindness, and that life's purpose will guide his extraordinary actions all the way to the moment of his death (Kaipa, 2014).

If you haven't found your north star yet, or have no idea what it might be, don't worry! It's never "too late" to discover your life's purpose. Furthermore, your north star may not be something that has to do with your career. Your north star could be becoming the best parent you can be to your children, or advocating for the environment, or amassing a fortune for retirement. There's no right or wrong life's purpose. The goal is to find something that's important enough to you to pursue with the same discipline and determination that the Spartans applied to their martial strength.

Finding your own north star is a journey, so give yourself some time to sit and think about what it might be. While you're discovering, there are five steps that you can follow to get yourself thinking about your north star and help you to uncover your true life's purpose (Ho, 2019).

1. **Break Free From Mental Limitations**

The first step in finding your north star is to silence the inner voice that tells you you aren't good enough to achieve the things you want to achieve. No matter what you want out of life, you have the ability to get it. It may take you a long time. It may require many difficult choices or years of hard work. But you *can* do it if it's worth it to you. When choosing your north star, then, it's time to forget rationalizations like "being realistic." Don't limit yourself to what's possible, because the point of choosing your north star is bending your willpower toward making it possible. Your journey through life is about discovering what is and isn't achievable for you. If you decide now that you don't have what it takes to get what you want, then you're stopping yourself before you've even started.

2. **Ask Yourself These Questions**

Take some time to sit with these questions. For some, the answers may come easily. Perhaps these are truths that you've buried under years of low self-esteem or social pressure. Others may take a while for you to answer. Perhaps you've never thought about these questions in a serious way before.

- What do you love to do?

Whether it's paint or drink beer or play ice hockey, just take a moment to think about the things that you truly love to do. Try not to frame this in terms of careers or professions or even social roles. Just think about the actions themselves. What activities, situations, or even people bring you the most joy in life?

- What activities set your soul on fire?

Ok, now take it up a notch. You might love drinking a cold beer on a summer's day, but does that activity set your soul on fire? Probably not. So now it's time to think about the things that you don't just love, but that fill you with a deep, all-consuming sense of passion. What really makes your blood flow and your heart sing? Which activities make you feel strong, capable, and powerful, even when you're faced with challenges or asked to learn something new?

- If money was no object, how would you spend your time?

If all of your basic needs were automatically met, what would your day look like? What are the things that you would devote your time to if you could? Too often, we rationalize giving up on our dreams because we have more practical matters in front of us that need to be met. And while working to pay your rent or feed your children is hardly something to be condemned, there are probably opportunities to pursue your dreams all around you that you've stopped looking for because you've convinced yourself that pursuing your dreams and meeting your basic needs are incompatible.

3. Think Back to When You Were a Child

What things brought you immense joy and satisfaction when you were a child? The individual activities might be different from the activities that bring you joy now, but you may notice some underlying similarities. More importantly, were there things that you loved to do as a child that adults told you to forget about? Were there dreams you expressed as a young person that were laughed off or condemned? Perhaps as a child you wanted to be an actor or a dancer or an astronaut, but someone convinced you that those goals weren't achievable for you. You may not want to be an actor or a dancer anymore, but there's probably something about those professions that still apply to your inner passions, something that you've spent your whole life telling yourself wasn't worth pursuing.

4. Spend Time in Contemplation

Give yourself a few minutes or even set aside a few hours to answer the questions above. Then continue to sit and think about them for a while. Give yourself a few days or even a few weeks to reflect on these questions. Observe yourself in your daily life. What makes you feel joy? What sacrifices of your time, energy, or money do you find yourself making that don't feel worth it? What inner goals or desires are those sacrifices holding you back from achieving?

5. Listen to That Feeling Deep in Your Bones

When you've found your north star, you'll know it. That can be a frustrating thing to hear, but it's true. When your mind finally alights on the thing that you would gladly devote your entire life to, you'll have a strong, electrifying feeling deep in your body. You know what your dreams are. You know what your passions are. The purpose of finding a north star is to uncover them. Once you've uncovered your true life's purpose, you can then set yourself the task of turning your dreams into real, achievable goals.

The Spartan Code

The Spartans paired their life's purpose with a strict code of honor, which they followed both in battle and in their daily lives. Every aspect of life in Sparta was geared toward the communal north star of having the finest military in the ancient world. The military was part of Spartan life, and Spartan life was ordered around the military. Arguably, no other culture in the history of the world has geared itself so totally around the achievement of greatness in one social aspect as Sparta did at the height of its military prowess (E., n.d.).

The basic formation in the Spartan military was called the *phalanx,* a tight formation of heavily armored soldiers. At the front of this formation, the soldiers would overlap their bronze shields in order to form a protective wall. They would then use their long spears to strike out at the enemy as the phalanx moved forward, or as enemies rushed the phalanx in an attempt to break it. But the phalanx was virtually indestructible. A tightly formed phalanx could defeat forces hundreds of times its size (E., n.d.).

The strength of the phalanx, however, had nothing to do with the material of the shields or the length of the spears. The strength of the phalanx lay in the strength of the formation. If even one warrior broke formation, it created an open spot, a place of weakness that the enemy could exploit. If all the soldiers in the phalanx remained firm and steadfast, then it was almost impossible for an enemy to break. The true strength of the Spartan military, therefore, lay not in the soldier's physical strength, but in their mental fortitude. It was their courage and determination to hold formation that made them the fiercest warriors of all time, not their technology, battle tactics, or physical strength (E., n.d.).

What made the phalanx and other battle tactics like it possible was the Spartan code of honor. No soldier was considered superior to any other. Spartan soldiers were expected to be heroic, and even to die if the needs of Sparta demanded that sacrifice. However, Spartans were also taught that they should fight always with the desire to live and fight again, and were certainly never expected to enter a battle without any regard for their own lives or personal safety. Suicidal recklessness, berserkery, and rage were strictly prohibited within the Spartan army because these kinds of behaviors endangered the phalanx. Stoic calmness was valued above all in a Spartan man, far more than blind battle rage. The more stoic and calm a warrior remained in the thick of battle, the more respect he earned from his fellow soldiers. It was stoic calmness that helped soldiers not to drop their shields or break the formation of the phalanx. But this same code also applied to Spartan men when they were off the battlefield. Spartans were expected to remain stoic and cool-headed at all times. Fits of rage or other emotions were frowned upon. Spartans were expected to remain in control of their emotions at all times, no matter what difficulties or uncertainties appeared before them (E., n.d.).

Remaining in control of one's emotions wasn't about ignoring or repressing them. It was about remaining *reliable.* Trust is the core of Spartan honor. Other people around you had to be able to rely on you to solve problems, overcome challenges, and support more vulnerable people through difficult moments. If you fell apart at the first sign of stress, then the people around you couldn't rely on you to pull through in difficult times. For the Spartans, being unreliable meant that you were dangerous. If others couldn't rely on you to hear or support them through their personal troubles, then they certainly couldn't rely on you to save their lives on the battlefield.

Today, what we can learn from this code is a sense of responsibility. Remember, responsibility and obligation are two different things. Obligation is when you put the needs of others before yours because you feel like you aren't worthy of care, success, or affection. But responsibility is when you put the needs of others before yours because you understand that, in that moment, that person's safety or well-being is dependent on your actions. When you act with responsibility, you give of yourself in the trust that the other person would do the same or even more for you. When you act out of obligation, however, you give of yourself without that trust, or perhaps even knowing that the other person is disproportionately taking from you.

To follow the Spartan code of honor, it's time to take a look at the sacrifices you make in your own life. When you act with concern for others, are you acting from a place of responsibility, or a place of obligation? When we make sacrifices from a sense of responsibility, we never feel regret or resentment. For example, we make a number of personal sacrifices for the safety and well-being of our children or our romantic partners. Making those sacrifices may be difficult or painful. We may have to make adjustments or ask for help along the way in order to better care for ourselves. But we never regret a sacrifice made for a loved one or for the sake of our life's purpose because we know that the pain was worth it.

Obligation, on the other hand, will eventually produce feelings of regret and resentment. If you find yourself feeling this way, it's time to take a step back and take a hard look at your life. What sacrifices fill you with resentment? Why do you feel obligated to make those sacrifices? What personal goals, priorities, or responsibilities are your obligations standing in the way of? And how would your life look different if you were to stand strong in support of the things that are truly important to you, rather than feeling pressured into acting contrary to your true responsibilities?

Finding your north star isn't just about finding your personal life's purpose. It's also about defining where your true responsibilities lie. There will always be people or situations in life that pressure you into acting outside of your best interests. There will always be times when you are being pressured to put your life's purpose aside for the sake of serving someone else's vision. Your north star will show you when sacrifice is a responsibility, and when sacrifice is being demanded as an obligation. Your north star will help you to make the sacrifices that are truly worth it, and prevent you from allowing others to use your strengths and talents for their personal gain.

In addition to discerning the difference between responsibility and obligation, there are two main takeaways we can apply from the Spartan code of honor to contemporary life. These lessons will help you to find something worth fighting for, remain true to what you believe in, and make the sacrifices that serve *your* life's purposes, rather than someone else's (K., 2014).

1. **Fear Shame**

Spartans eventually grew up with an intense fear of shame. This fear of shame is part of why their upbringing was so brutal, but it was effective in motivating them to commit to honorable and responsible actions. Enlist shame as a kind of emotional armor against fear. Make yourself more afraid of letting yourself or others down than you are of oncoming change, pain, or discomfort. This is how many Spartan soldiers pushed themselves to do things that they never believed possible. In a way, the Spartan culture of shame was the most intense form of community support. Imagine if pursuing your true life's goals was seen by those around you as the only option, and anything less was viewed as intensely shameful.

2. Embrace Hardship

Though our contemporary world often equates comfort with success, the reality is that there is no such thing as a truly comfortable life. In fact, too much comfort can often lead to depression, because too much comfort typically means a cessation of growth. Often, the things that we employ purely for the sake of convenience or making our lives "easier" end up making our lives more complicated because comfort, by itself, isn't a healthy life goal.

Our modern world tends to prioritize routine over physical effort, physical effort over mental effort, and mental effort over mental clarity. We pursue things that make our lives easier, mistakenly believing that making things easier means making things more efficient. But eliminating actions or discomfort doesn't always improve productivity, and it certainly won't make you happy. The Spartans understood that true excellence comes from the pursuit of better actions, not better things.

A great illustration of this is the Spartan story of the defeat of the Persians at Platea in 479 BCE. The spoils of the battle included all of the Persian king's cooks, wine stewards, and kitchen staff. After the battle, the Spartan king asked the Persian cooks to prepare the same kind of meal they would have prepared for their king, and asked his own cooks to prepare a typical Spartan meal.

The Persians ended up serving a lavish feast, serving multiple courses of delicacies on golden plates. The Spartan cooks, on the other hand, served a traditional Spartan meal of barley bread and pig's blood stew. When the Spartans saw the two meals served together, they burst out laughing. The Spartan king famously remarked "How far the Persians have traveled to rob us of our poverty!"

The Spartans didn't see the feast as some great reward, because their purpose in defeating the Persians wasn't about gaining material wealth. Their focus was on honor and personal growth, not on riches or spoils. They were so focused, in fact, that they took more pleasure in *rejecting* the feast than they took in eating it.

The lesson to be learned here is that hardship doesn't have to be hard. When you become fully focused on achieving a certain goal or purpose, then physical pleasures become relegated to trivialities and distractions.

Chapter 4:

How to Rid Your Life of Those Pesky Distractions

Once you've found your north star, it then becomes important to focus on how to minimize the potential for destruction within your life. Like a farmer building a fence around his crops, it's important for us to build healthy barriers and boundaries within our minds. In today's world, distractions are everywhere, to the point that keeping them at bay can feel impossible even for the most mentally resilient people. However, there are a few practical things we can do to minimize the mental chaos that distractions cause.

Today's world is very different from the one the Spartans lived in. One of the major differences between our world and the world of the Spartans is the abundance of distractions that the contemporary person faces on a daily basis. The Internet, mobile phones, news apps, and an increased sense of global connectedness are just a few of the places from which distractions are coming at us all day long (and often all night long as well).

The Spartans understood that the ability to remain focused is critical to your success or failure. Without focus, you can't get anything done. And if you can't get anything done, then accomplishing even the smallest of goals will become impossible. Whether your distractions are electronic, interpersonal, or internal, there are a few mental tricks that contemporary people have developed to build resilience against them (Daskal, 2020).

Check Up On Yourself

As always, the first place to start is within yourself. If you find yourself mentally scattered, take a moment to ask yourself what's really going on. What's causing you to feel so scatterbrained or anxious? What do you need to be thinking about or working on right now, and what's really stopping you from devoting your full attention to what's in front of you?

Pinpoint the Cause

Once you've determined potential internal sources of distraction, only then is it time to look outward for external causes. Is there something about your office set-up or an intrusive coworker that's stopping you from remaining focused on what you need to be working on? Perhaps you don't have the skills, ideas, or time to complete the task in front of you. Perhaps you're simply burned out, and the best thing you can do to achieve your goal is (paradoxically) to take a break from it. Once you've identified the cause, you can then start to take the right actions to solve it and eliminate or minimize that distraction in the future.

Be Prepared

Having a plan is crucial to success, because if you know what you're doing next, then you never have a moment of hesitation. It's in moments when we're uncertain or when the next step is unclear that we are most vulnerable to distractions. So when a task or project comes your way, make sure you take a moment to break it down into small, sequential steps. Make sure you know every step that must be taken to accomplish the task from start to finish, and give each step a deadline. Sometimes you can't know everything in advance, and unexpected circumstances will always arise. Making a plan isn't about rigidly sticking to it; it's about knowing what comes next so that distractions don't have the power to sidetrack you. Think of the popular business adage: 10 minutes of planning saves an hour of execution.

Go Offline

The biggest sources of distraction we face in the contemporary world come in the form of email, social media, and cell phones. Though Internet and digital resources can be beneficial, the only way to truly focus is to take yourself offline until you've finished the task in front of you. The potential for distraction that comes from cell phones and social media in particular can do a lot of damage to your attention span. Keep yourself offline as much as possible when you're working, and you'll find your ability to focus greatly improved.

Give Yourself a Break

Knowing when to take breaks is key to success. Our productivity-driven society loves to praise people who work 60 hour work weeks and skip their lunch breaks, but the reality is that your brain can only focus for so long. Sometimes becoming easily distracted is just a sign that your brain needs a break. Pausing for even just 10 minutes can help your brain to recharge and refocus. Don't look at breaks as rewards—look at them as moments to care for your brain to keep your thoughts sharp.

Tune It Out

Silence is often touted as ideal for a workspace, but there's been a great deal of research to suggest that music actually helps to improve focus. It's not only a brain thing; playing background music or putting on headphones helps you to tune out other sounds that might potentially distract you, such as conversations, irritating construction, or any other unpleasant sounds in your work environment. Not only does the music itself help you concentrate, but headphones are a signal to other people that you are concentrating right now, which can also serve to minimize the distractions that come from other people.

Break It Down

If you're finding yourself extra distracted, try breaking down the tasks in front of you into even smaller pieces. The simpler and more achievable the task in front of you is, the easier it will be to force yourself to remain focused and get it done. The more mini-tasks you achieve, the more motivated you will be to push through to the end of the bigger, more important tasks on your to-do list.

Clean It Up

Though many people don't like to hear this, the quality of your workspace has a direct impact on your ability to focus. "Organized" looks different to different people, but if you find yourself constantly unable to find important documents or running late for pre-scheduled meetings, then it's time to take a look at your system. Organizing doesn't just mean the physical surface of your desk or office space, either. The way that your digital files are organized (or not) can also have a real impact on your ability to focus and get things done.

Set a Deadline

Whenever possible, give yourself a deadline whenever you take on a new task or project. When you break down projects into small steps or plan out your day, estimate how much time it's going to take you to complete each task, and then give yourself an extra 30 minutes. Giving yourself a deadline helps to keep you motivated and on-track, but over-scheduling yourself can also cause you to feel distracted and anxious. Give yourself reasonable, achievable deadlines for each of your tasks. If you finish early, you can reward yourself with a break, or you can give yourself that much more time to complete the next task on your schedule.

Become an Early Bird

If at all possible, try starting your workday an hour before everyone else. Getting started an hour early gives you time in silence and solitude to organize your day, get yourself mentally prepared to start your work, and even get a headstart on important tasks before your coworkers arrive in the office. For similar reasons, it can also be beneficial to skip the long office lunches in the middle of the day. If at all possible, give yourself multiple, short breaks throughout the day instead of carving out an hour in the middle for lunch. Frequent breaks will help to keep your mind sharp throughout the day, rather than watching your productivity decrease dramatically the closer you get to lunch hour. Replacing your lunch hour with frequent, shorter breaks quite literally saves you both time and energy, ensuring that your brain gets the rest that it needs to continue working while maximizing the time you spend at work.

Put Yourself in Distraction-Free Mode

By applying all of the above strategies to your daily work, you begin to create habits that help your brain to automatically eliminate distractions and stay focused. First and foremost, start by creating a work environment in which you're less tempted to become preoccupied with things that aren't important. Depending on the nature of your work, or the nature of the task you're trying to focus on, this isn't always easy, but it's crucial to maintaining focus. One major obstacle for the 21st century worker is that most of our distractions come from the Internet, but most of us also need a computer to get our work done. One useful tool that many people use to keep themselves off of video-streaming or shopping websites when they're supposed to be working is website blocker apps. Essentially, the app will prevent you from accessing certain sites within a certain period of time (Patel, 2018).

Another important environmental distraction comes from the people around us. Finding simple ways to signal to others that you can't be disturbed can free you from a great deal of distraction. If you have a door to close, close it when you're trying to focus. Headphones are another easy way to signal to others that you're trying to focus.

Turn off your phone or put it on silent when you're working to minimize potential distractions coming to you in the form of text messages or app notifications. If you work in an open office, you may want to see if there is another, quieter location you can move to when you really need to concentrate. Studies have found that those working in an open office are 64% more likely to become distracted throughout the workday. While this may not be surprising, it's also true that open office plans are more common than closed or private office spaces.

These are all small but important ways that you can close yourself off from distractions or excuses not to work, and help you to remain focused on the task that's right in front of you (Patel, 2018).

Breaking It Down

Finding your north star is about discovering your life's purpose, but maintaining focus is the grunt work that you have to put in every day to keep yourself on track. One easy way to remain focused on your big life goals is to break them down into smaller, sub-goals. Then break those goals down into smaller pieces, and break those pieces down into still smaller pieces, until you've broken your north star down into a series of daily tasks and responsibilities.

Visualization is a useful and important tactic for maintaining focus as well. Whenever you're planning your day or setting new goals for yourself, visualize yourself completing each task smoothly and competently. This isn't about setting yourself up with unrealistic expectations; it's about imagining yourself being successful. It's very easy to imagine yourself failing or imagine all the things that can go wrong when we set out to complete a task. Imagining that everything is unfolding exactly as it should is something that we have to actively remind ourselves to do, because believing in our own potential is critical to our success.

There are some practical ways that you can break your north star down into smaller, achievable goals (and achieve them). But before trying to put those tips into practice, there are some simple truths to accept about distraction.

First, **avoiding distraction is tough.** This is where Spartan discipline comes in. Sticking to your goals requires a certain level of mental steel. It often means saying no to opportunities to have fun or take it easy, and it often means saying yes to opportunities to work hard or make sacrifices. Keeping an eye on your north star helps to remind you *why* you're doing what you're doing, but discipline is how you make yourself actually do it (Mires, 2020).

Second, **you were never taught how to focus.** All throughout your education, was there ever a moment when a teacher stopped and actually taught you how to pay attention or remain free of distractions? Probably not, but you were certainly expected to do it anyway. But focus is a skill like any other, and if you don't pick up on it naturally, that doesn't mean that you're inherently a distractible person. Learning how to focus requires practice, and if it's something that you aren't used to, then applying focus techniques is going to be uncomfortable at first. Remember, being uncomfortable doesn't mean that you're doing something wrong. It just means that you're doing something new (Mires, 2020).

Third, **everyone uses different tools for maintaining focus.** Though this chapter will walk you through some strategies that many people use to help them focus, that doesn't mean that these strategies will all work for you. Everyone's brain, life purpose, life circumstances, and working environment is different. That means that the things that help someone else focus may not necessarily work for you. You might have to make some adjustments or try a few different strategies before you find the ones that really work for you. Don't be afraid to do some experimenting, and be patient with yourself.

And now, some practical tips for breaking your north star down into smaller, more achievable goals…

Keep Your Vision and Goals in Mind

Don't break your north star down so much that you lose sight of the big picture. Why do you even need to focus in the first place? What's so important about completing this task anyway? Whether your goal is to become a great guitar player, write a novel, or successfully make a living working from home, always remember why you want to achieve that goal in the first place. Remember always how these goals are serving your greater life's purpose. Keep yourself focused on why you want to achieve these things in the first place, and that will give you the discipline you need to get through the tough and tedious aspects of achieving those goals. When things get difficult and boring is when we're most vulnerable to distraction (Mires, 2020).

Reduce the Chaos of Your Day and Prioritize Two or Three Important Tasks

Especially in today's world, it's far too easy to over-schedule ourselves. But realistically, there's no way you can look at a 20-item to-do list and not feel distracted. No matter how hard you try, you can't expect yourself to achieve anything with sophistication if you're trying to juggle too many items at the same time, or if you're racing through your tasks at breakneck speed because you've scheduled yourself more items than you realistically have the time or energy to finish. Without a doubt, there are many things on your to-do list that aren't serving your life's purpose, and therefore aren't worth your mental energy.

When planning your day, give yourself no more than three tasks. Ask yourself, "If I could only get three things done today, what would those three things be?" This will force you to prioritize the three things that matter the most, and at the end of the day, three items is all you need to keep yourself moving slowly and steadily toward your goals. Better still, you'll find yourself completing those tasks at a higher level of excellence, you'll feel much more secure and confident in your ability to complete those tasks, and you'll probably find yourself finishing them faster because you're more focused. If you finish your three items with time to spare, then you can make the choice to take it easy, or set yourself three more tasks. Regardless, over-scheduling yourself is a sure way to burn yourself out (Mires, 2020).

Do Important Tasks as Soon as Possible

Setting yourself just three tasks a day doesn't mean you're now free to surf social media until noon before you start your day. Once you've chosen your three tasks for the day, get started on the first one as soon as possible. Eventually, you'll get yourself in the mental habit of starting to plan your day and prioritize your task-list as soon as you get out of bed in the morning. Wake up, use the bathroom, eat breakfast, and start planning your day. If you can plan and set your three daily tasks before you get to work, so much the better. The moment you sit down at your desk, you can get straight to work.

Though disciplining yourself in this way can be tough, waiting to get your day started only makes you more vulnerable to distraction. If you aren't actively working on a task, then distractions will present themselves, and the more distractions you expose yourself to, the more likely you are to spend your precious time and energy on them instead of on the things that are most important. Setting yourself three tasks a day isn't about giving you more time to hang around, it's about sharpening your mental focus so that you can accomplish those tasks with the maximum amount of skill.

Focus On the Smallest Tasks First

An alternative method is to break your big goals down into very small, but very achievable, steps. If you follow this method, you may very well find yourself with a 20-item to-do list, but those 20-items are all extremely small, simple tasks. Most goals that are truly worth pursuing can't be done in 24-hours. They often take weeks or even months to accomplish. Looking at goals from this perspective can sometimes make them seem overwhelmingly big, to the point that you lose your willpower to get started on them. The two easiest ways to kill your discipline are to either become discouraged by the size of your goal, or to start fantasizing about how good you'll feel when the goal has been accomplished. Both mindsets take you out of the present moment, and therefore cause you to become more distracted. Focus means looking at the very first, smallest step, the one that is right in front of you.

For example, imagine that you want to become a great writer. Rather than looking at the monstrous goal of writing an entire novel, set yourself a minimum goal of two sentences a day. Two sentences is certainly manageable, right? So manageable that you'll often find yourself overshooting that goal by thousands of words a day. But if you set yourself the goal of writing 200 (or 2,000) words a day, you might get too discouraged to write anything at all (Mires, 2020).

Visualization

If you find yourself fantasizing about what your life will look like after you've accomplished your goal, stop yourself. Instead, imagine yourself completing the task that's currently in front of you. Don't imagine yourself succeeding, imagine yourself actually working. Athletes of all kinds use this tactic to keep themselves grounded in the game, race, or competition ahead. They don't imagine themselves winning the game, they just imagine themselves (successfully) making the next play.

So for example, if it's time for you to practice guitar and you find yourself procrastinating, take a moment to imagine yourself unpacking your guitar and playing the chords or practicing the song that you've set for yourself today. It might seem like a silly thing to do, but visualizing yourself working serves to keep your brain focused on the task at hand, and "preps the body" for the task it's about to complete. In this way, imagining yourself completing the task makes it that much easier for you to get started (Mires, 2020).

Control your Internal Distractions

Not all distractions are external. In fact, many of our distractions come from non-essential thoughts within our own minds while we're trying to work. This is why preparing your mind for work is such a crucial part of any focus-based work routine. Small signals to your brain that it's time to work help your brain start to automatically adjust its thought processes to eliminate stray or extraneous thoughts.

One common trick for mental work prep is to set yourself a dedicated work space. If you always work in a certain place, then your mind will automatically start to prepare itself for work whenever you enter that space. This is relatively easy when you have a desk or an office, but make sure that when you take breaks, you leave your desk or workspace in order to take them. This makes the distinction between work and rest more clear, and gives your mind permission to wander freely when you're on break.

Deadlines are another good way to manage internal distractions. Whenever you feel your mind wandering, remind yourself of the time or date that your current task is due. This will give you a little rush of adrenaline, which will subsequently give your brain a little chemical boost that it needs to get back to work.

Above all, the key to managing internal distractions is to not give them a lot of power. When you find your thoughts wandering, gently pull yourself back to the task at hand. Maybe get up and go for a walk or take a five minute coffee break. Maybe remind yourself of a looming deadline or pause for a moment to visualize yourself completing the task at hand. What you shouldn't do is get flustered or frustrated with yourself. Wandering thoughts are perfectly normal, but if you allow yourself to get annoyed with yourself, then you're only contributing to your inability to work. Getting frustrated is a sure way to kill your productivity (Mires, 2020).

Focus on Staying Focused

For many people, it's easy to stay focused by putting their energy toward eliminating distractions. But for other people, distractions are inevitable or out of their control. If this is you, then your energies will be better spent focusing on…well, on focusing. Instead of looking at your environment or the world around you for potential distractions, try these mental exercises to keep your mind focused and sharp no matter what the world around you looks like (Lane, 2016).

Take Stock

Designate one day a week that you spend simply planning, prioritizing, and organizing. Identify all the distractions that come your way during the week, and determine which ones are eating up the most of your time. This will help you to focus your mental energies on resolving the distractions that are most pressing, and stop you from expending any more unnecessary mental energy on distractions that aren't major or are entirely out of your control.

Prioritize Your To-Do List

However you organize your to-do list, identify the two tasks that are most important and move them to the top of the list. Think about it this way: if you could only get two things on your list done today, what would those two things be? This will automatically motivate you to get the most important items on your list done. Once those two items are done, you'll find it much easier to focus on the others because the most important and pressing work of the day is already behind you.

Divide Your Workday into 60-90 Minute Blocks

Your brain can only focus for so long. At some point, you need a break. The more frequently you can take breaks, the more productive you'll be when you get back to work. Many people have found it useful to break their day into 60 or even 90 minute chunks of work, followed by a short ten or fifteen minute break. If at all possible, break up your workday into these chunks. Though it might feel odd to be constantly starting and stopping, you'll probably find that you get a lot more work done in an hour after you've taken a 10 minute break than you get done in three or four hours without any break at all.

Schedule Your Distractions

They're going to happen anyway, so why not put them into your schedule as breaks? Especially if you follow the 60-90 minute rule, give yourself 10 or 15 minutes to engage in the activities that once were invasive distractions. When you take stock of your more pervasive distractions, work on how to schedule the more pressing ones into your schedule. Whether it's chit-chatting with coworkers, surfing social media, or getting a snack from the vending machines, rather than trying to resist these temptations entirely, simply move them to your next scheduled 10 or 15 minute break block.

Say No to Checking Your Email

Unfortunately, many jobs use email or business chat platforms in order to facilitate workplace communications. This is unfortunate because it creates yet another source for distractions to come at us throughout the workday. Almost all of the emails we receive on a daily basis are not urgent, but it's easy to feel like they are. Constantly checking our email throughout the day may actually feel productive, but in reality, it's yet another distraction keeping us from focusing on the tasks that are truly important. To break yourself of this destructive habit, set aside pre-scheduled time throughout the day to check and answer email correspondences. Many highly successful business people set aside a half hour in the morning and the half hour before their workday ends to email. This might seem like a long time to wait, but what it does is free up time throughout the day for you to focus on tasks that are more important. Someone who emails you in the middle of the day can probably wait a few hours for you to answer them back, and if they can't, that probably reflects more on them than it does on you.

Put Down the Phone

As with email, unsolicited phone calls or text messages throughout the day are rarely relevant to the two or three most important tasks on your priority list. When these notifications do come through, we feel compelled to answer them right away, but the truth is that these, too, are distractions that pull us away from the work that's truly important. When you're working, turn off your phone or put it on silent. You can push cell phone time to your designated break times.

Close Your Internet Browser

Many of us need computers to do our daily work, but that means that it's all too easy to open Facebook or Twitter to surf social media when you should be working. Social media is perhaps the number one distraction that contemporary humans face, sapping time and energy that we could (and should) be spending on the things that are really important to us. If you want to remain fully focused, do whatever you have to do to keep yourself off of social media during work hours. Relegating social media time to your breaks is a good motivator to put yourself on a brain-friendly schedule, and you can even use social media time as a reward to motivate yourself to push through necessary tasks that are boring or difficult.

Make Your Intentions Known

If you're committed to being more productive or have newly discovered your north star, don't be shy about letting the people around you know. One of the biggest benefits of the Spartan model of success was that everyone in the community was focused on achieving the same goal. We don't have the same luxury in today's more liberal world, but that doesn't mean that the people around you can't support you in achieving your life's purpose. Whatever modifications you've decided to make to your schedule or lifestyle in order to achieve your goals should be shared with the people around you. Those who support you living your life to the fullest will understand and respect your boundaries if you tell them that you're not going to be available to chat at certain times of the day. It doesn't necessarily mean expecting that others are going to rearrange their lives around your needs. It just means letting the ones you love know that you're taking your commitments and goals seriously. Those who truly support you will be glad to wait until your designated break times to chat or share memes on Instagram.

Wear Headphones

The power of music to improve concentration has only recently been understood by scientists. Better still, headphones send a clear message to people around you that you aren't socially available right now. Listening to music has the advantage of increasing the amount of endorphins in your brain, which increases your sense of pleasure and happiness, even if the task you're performing is boring or unpleasant. It also eliminates potentially distracting or unpleasant noises from your environment, and it eliminates social distractions by gently letting the people around you know that now is not the right time to chit chat.

Move to Another Location

Not all office spaces, unfortunately, are ideally set up for maximum workplace focus. If at all possible, see if there's a conference room or unused office where you can relocate during times of extreme concentration. If you work at home, try to find a room with a door you can close or where other people are unlikely to disturb you. The kitchen table, for example, isn't an ideal workspace because it's a communal space where other people might be relaxing, socializing, or preparing food for themselves while you're trying to work.

If You Have a Door, Shut It

A surprising number of people who complain about workplace distractions have a door that they could shut; they just choose not to. Too many of us feel that closing the door while we're at work is rude, but the opposite is true. If you leave your door open when you need to concentrate, you're putting yourself in the way of distractions and you're sending a false invitation to those around you. Closing the door is actually the *polite* way to signal to others that you can't be disturbed right now.

Delegate

The Spartans had a very low tolerance for heroics, and so should you. There's no reason for you to be working extra hours or taking on extra projects that you know you can't handle. Stop trying to be the hero, and be honest about what you can actually achieve with the time and energy that you have. If you have too much on your plate, learn how to delegate. Say no to extra projects that come your way when your schedule is already full. Pass off small or simple tasks to coworkers that can handle it. Trying to juggle more than you're capable of handling only decreases your productivity, and that, in turn, decreases the productivity of those around you.

Remove External Distractions

Sometimes we convince ourselves that we have "no control" over certain external distractions. But if the television is a distraction and your wife/family member/roommate just won't turn it off, you could always move to another room. If the kids distract you in the morning, try waking up an hour before they do. If the Internet is a distraction, download a website blocking app or even turn off your modem while you're working. Don't allow external distractions to prevent you from achieving things that are important to you. Circumstances in which you can't do *anything* to change your situation are much more rare than you might think. Nine times out of ten, there's something that you can do. So swallow your pride, stop whining, and do it.

Chapter 5:

Creativity On Demand

Once we have the right barriers in place, as well as a solid foundation in existence beneath them, we want to do what we can to ensure this mental foundation can perform to its fullest potential on demand. In order to bypass distraction and push through discomfort, you need an arsenal of mental and emotional tools that will help you do just that at a moment's notice, no matter what situation you find yourself in. Once you've started taking steps to eliminate distractions and improve your focus, the next step is to get yourself into a mental state where you aren't just focused, you're inspired.

The important thing to remember about creativity is that it is yet another learnable, trainable mental skill. It's not a personality trait, and for most people, it's not something that you're born with. There are a few select individuals who find themselves naturally bursting with creative ideas. But for the rest of us, creativity is something that we need to practice in order to become good at. And before you dismiss creativity as the province of "flighty" types like artists or poets, consider that creativity is a skill that all people need in order to succeed. Creativity is what helps us to solve problems. It's what helps us to try new things or experiment with new solutions. Creativity simply means feeling empowered to do things your own way, whether that's writing a novel, designing a website, or simply having the courage to mess around with the pipes under the sink until the water pressure goes back to normal.

Moving through tough mental situations is a lot easier if you have a toolbox of mental skills that you can use should the situation require it. There are a number of different mental skills you can practice on a daily basis until they become habits, or automatic responses that you can enlist when appropriate to the specific emotional challenge in front of you (Grenny, 2019).

Frame the Problem

Know what the issue is, and then take a mental step back. Let it sit in your subconscious for a few days, without forcing yourself to come up with a solution right away. When the moment of inspiration finally comes, don't hesitate to act. Cognitive irritation is a great way to foster creativity. When you give yourself a compelling and complex, but unresolved, problem, your brain becomes irritated. After all, our brains are wired to solve problems, and to be uncomfortable with unknowns and uncertainties. Use this to your advantage. Your brain will first try to take the easiest way out, so allow yourself to consider the first round of possibilities, all of which will be unsatisfying if you're working toward something that's important to you. Be patient with yourself. Once you've worked through the easy solutions, your brain will truly be ready to tackle the problem head-on. The important skill to foster is not forcing the issue. If you really can't think of any answers right now, table the problem and move to the next task on your to-do list. All day (and night) long, your brain will be subconsciously working on the problem. More often than not, the solution will come when you least expect it, when your brain is fully relaxed and therefore better able to think clearly.

Obey Your Curiosity

If something sounds like it might interest you, investigate. When new ideas and interests are firing inside your head is the moment when you're most creative. Use this to your advantage. Steve Jobs once famously said that true creativity is "just" the act of "connecting things." So give yourself permission to make those connections. More importantly, expose yourself to more ideas that you can connect. Honoring passing curiosities is the best way to build a solid mental database of information.

If something strikes your fancy or ignites your interest, give yourself a moment to indulge and explore. Follow paths that have no obvious purpose. Simply satisfying a whim is reason enough to pursue something that's interesting to you. Whether it's an article online, a panel at a conference, a book on the shelf, or even another person who's caught your attention, give yourself permission to indulge your interest. Honor your curiosity. Your interest is a signal from your brain that this is something that could be relevant to your life's purpose. The information or experience that you glean may not be relevant now, but you have no idea how it's going to be useful later on. Honoring your curiosity is investing in your creative and intellectual potential. Squashing your curiosity only ultimately serves to stifle your creative growth.

Keep a Shoebox

This doesn't have to be literal, but find some method of recording or saving items or experiences that are meaningful to you. For example, if you're constantly finding information in books that strikes you emotionally or intellectually, invest in a good highlighter or start writing things down. Find some way to collect and preserve the things that strike your interest. Collecting interesting items or information might seem obsessive at first, but there's going to be a point down the line when you'll want to go back and revisit that moment, information, or experience. This will ultimately help you to make the "connections" that Steve Jobs was talking about. When you read something or hear something that reminds you of an experience you had or something else that you read, it's going to be much better for your creative mind if you can easily recall the past experience and make those connections.

Pursue the Uncomfortable

This is definitely Spartan advice, but it's wisdom that's followed by creative thinkers in all disciplines today. Doing things that you don't like doing is the best possible way to push yourself out of your comfort zone. Having the conversation that you've been dreading for weeks or reading articles about subjects you aren't typically interested in might seem painful at first, but what they will ultimately do is force you to think in ways you've never had to think before. More often than not, the things that we label as "boring" are just things that we don't understand. Taking the time to invest a little intellectual energy in a subject may be all we need to understand, and subsequently unlock an entirely new way of thinking that was previously closed off to us.

Have Uncomfortable Conversations

If you're dreading having a certain conversation that you know you need to have, set yourself a deadline for ripping off the proverbial band-aid. More often than not, the most intellectually stimulating conversations are the ones we have with people with whom we would normally avoid engaging. Painful or difficult conversations won't necessarily change your mind or sway your beliefs, but what they will do is expand your understanding of the world. Difficult conversations are difficult because they force us to see the world from a new perspective, and consider ideas that we previously were resistant to accepting. The more practice you have in grappling with other people's realities, the better you will be in understanding the perspectives of others. The more easily you can understand different kinds of people, the more easily you will be able to navigate difficult social situations or necessary interpersonal conflict.

Stop and Work

If you find yourself inspired, don't try to save or savor the moment. As any great writer or thinker will tell you, the idea won't last if you don't act immediately. I even have a writer friend who keeps a notebook on the bathroom sink when they take a shower. He won't even wait the extra five to ten minutes to soap up before writing down a good idea, because he knows that good ideas can disappear just as easily as they appear. The most important part of fostering a creative mind is to *act* on that creativity.

Write down your good ideas. Pull out your sketch pad or your camera when you feel compelled to capture an interesting visual moment. If you find yourself suddenly struck with an idea on how to pitch your idea to the board or how to navigate an upcoming surgery, do what you need to do to preserve your idea. Write it down, record yourself on your phone, or simply call up a friend to work through your new idea out-loud. Whatever you do, don't let the moment of inspiration pass.

Embrace All Ideas - Including the Bad Ones

How often have you been in a meeting or a classroom where the room was invited to ask questions or share ideas? And how often have you had an idea or a question, but chosen to remain silent? This choice to keep quiet is, more often than not, a fear response. Specifically, it's a reaction to the fear of looking foolish. But bad ideas are part of the creative process. Perhaps you'll look foolish, but what you'll learn from putting your bad idea out into the world will almost always be valuable enough to counteract the momentary embarrassment that comes with realizing your idea wasn't as brilliant as you originally thought (T., 2019).

Keeping silent is counterproductive to creativity. Holding yourself back is a sure way to kill your creative spark. You might think your idea is obvious, silly, or outlandish, but you don't know until you've given it a try. Perhaps your idea *is* obvious, silly, or outlandish, but it might also be the thing that sparks a creative idea in another person, or even sparks another, more productive idea within yourself.

Mental Exercises for Sparking Creativity

While there are certain mental habits that are beneficial to get into for nurturing creativity, there are other habits that you can actively pursue on a daily basis. Attempting to work these mental exercises into your everyday life will flex your creative muscles, and eventually get you into the habit of thinking creatively whenever the need arises (T., 2019).

Seek New Experiences (And Don't Forget to Record Them)

The best thing you can do to expand and ignite your creative faculties is to put yourself in new situations. Travelling, reading, and meeting new people are perhaps the easiest ways to expose yourself to new ideas, new situations, and new challenges, all of which are fertile ground in which to indulge your curiosity and expand your creative skillset. Every time you encounter a new situation or push yourself to solve a new problem, you're expanding on your creative toolbox, gradually widening your skillset until you have an automatic set of mental skills that you can bring to any problem you encounter.

But the best way to reap the maximum creative benefit from new situations is to record your experiences in some way. Writing things down, taking pictures, or even saving physical mementos from certain experiences can provide valuable insight for you when you reflect on them later. Your thoughts may be half-formed in the moment, but eventually you'll encounter a new situation that reminds you of a past experience, or gives you new insight into a problem or situation that you encountered in the past. Collecting small mementos to remind you of significant moments will make it easier for you to reflect on those moments when they become relevant in the future, and help you to build the mental connections that are the foundation of creative thought.

Get Out of Your Comfort Zone

If you learn nothing else from the Spartan mindset, learn that comfort is the enemy of creative thought. Exposing yourself to the unknown stimulates your mind and necessitates the formation of new ideas or perspectives. Embracing the uncomfortable puts you in unexpected situations and forces you to expand your understanding of how the world works. The more unknowns you expose yourself to, the more "knowns" you have stored away in your personal experiences to draw upon for future reference. The more of the world you expose yourself to, the bigger your worldview becomes.

Encourage yourself to talk to people who seemingly have nothing in common with you, to investigate topics that you know nothing about, and to expose yourself to groups or ideologies that you are intellectually or even morally opposed to. The information that you gain from these very uncomfortable exposures will help you to bridge the gap between the familiar and the unfamiliar, between the known and the unknown. Intentionally exposing yourself to things that you don't know anything about or even that you actively dislike gives you more mental clarity, providing a good opportunity for personal introspection and helping you to interact with ideas or perspectives that you've never previously considered.

Give Yourself Space

Always remember that creativity isn't always something we can call up on demand. Sometimes we need time to think. Sometimes we need the right space in which to think. The more you respect your creative process, the more you'll start to learn the types of environments and situations that truly free up your creative faculties. When the problem demands it, you'll slowly become more comfortable turning off your phone, going for a walk, or otherwise changing your surroundings in order to encourage the flow of creative energy when you're working out a particularly difficult project or problem.

Some people benefit creatively from environments that are quiet or remote, but others find that they get their best work done in noisy cafes or even on public transit. The trick is to find the right mental space that gives you the freedom to sit with new ideas without any external interruptions, pressures, or judgements. The more you can put your workspace in alignment with this type of environment, the more fertile your creative mind will be when you're at work.

Get Mad

Another great way to become creative is to get yourself into a healthy venting state. When you have lots to complain about, that means that you see lots of potential problems that could be fixed. Harness your frustration and anger. Use it as fuel for your creative energy. Rather than wallowing, try channeling that energy into something productive and constructive. If only the people in power would just *listen* to you, how would you solve the problem that's driving you absolutely crazy? Once you've vented away your feelings of anger, take a moment to look objectively at your "ideal" solutions. What real, practical steps can you take to turn these hypothetical changes into reality?

Keep Your Brain Full

Turn your distractions to your advantage. Never turn off or discourage your creativity. Allow yourself to go down rabbit holes and explore new information, whether or not it seems directly relevant to your current project. Sometimes your brain needs a "break" from the task at hand in order to think clearly. Instead of doing something mindless, however, see if you can get yourself engaged in something different. The more ideas are floating around in your head at any one time, the more likely you are to make the right connections that you need to spark a creative solution to your current problem.

Books, blogs, music, art, movies, TV shows, and videos are all great ways to both train and relax your brain at the same time. Engaging with any of these activities doesn't require any creative output from you, which is why they feel more relaxing than actually writing your own book or blog would feel. However, all of these media are full of information, emotion, and ideas that are still stimulating for your brain, giving it new thoughts to explore and new information to store for later.

If you find yourself stumped, don't be afraid to give yourself a creative "break" by engaging with other media. The important part is making sure that the content you're putting into your brain is interesting, stimulating, and beneficial. It doesn't necessarily have to be related to the project that you're currently working on, but if it's not engaging, then it's not giving you any new ideas. The more you can get in the habit of relaxing with creatively stimulating media instead of "mindless" media that doesn't interest you or excite your curiosity, the more interesting thoughts and perspectives you'll have stored in your brain for future use (Dixon, 2018).

Keep a Wheel Book

A wheel book is essentially a place where you store new information that you encounter throughout the day that you find interesting or emotionally stimulating. This could be a physical notebook, a voice recorder, or even an app on your smartphone. Regardless of the form it takes, the important thing is that the wheel book is something you can carry with you at all times. Whether it's a line from an article, a beautiful image, or something interesting that someone said in conversation, put anything and everything that interests you throughout the day in your wheel book. This will do two things for your brain.

First, it will get you in the mental habit of paying attention to the world around you. Rather than floating through life in a fog, your brain will be awake and aware of all the interesting things that happen around you all the time. Second, recording interesting things makes you more likely to remember them. When you're truly in a creative slump, you'll have a personal library of interesting ideas to look back through to get your brain fired up again (Dixon, 2018).

Create More Downtime

Breaks are an extremely undervalued part of the creative process. Downtime is when your brain subconsciously works through all the ideas and information that it's been exposed to throughout the day. This is why great ideas so often come to us when we're in the shower or on a long drive. Paradoxically, it's sometimes when your brain is fully relaxed that it is able to make the connections that you can't force it to make when you're sitting at your desk actively engaged in a project.

This is why scheduling yourself regular, small breaks throughout the day is so good for your mind, especially if you're engaged in some kind of creative work. Those brief periods of rest give your brain time to work through the information that you just processed in your last hour of work. When you come back to your desk to get ready to work again, you'll find yourself bursting with insights and good ideas, whereas if you had simply powered straight through two hours of work, you'd probably find yourself feeling burned out and frustrated (Dixon, 2018).

Be Still

An extreme version of creating downtime is intentionally scheduling time during the day to be in both stillness and silence. Meditation, journaling, and photography are all good ways to program stillness into your daily routine. Even just fifteen minutes a day of these activities gives your brain an extreme moment of rest. It gives your brain a moment to process all the input it has received throughout the day without giving it anything new to process. Moments of stillness are pure moments of rest, moments when your only intention is to care for your brain and get it back up and running.

Creativity Is Always There

Everyone has the ability to be creative, but in order to truly get into a creative flow, your brain has to be focused. And in order to be focused, you have to be free of distractions—or at least, as free as you can be. As you start to learn how to minimize and eliminate distractions from your life, you'll find your mind becoming much sharper. Most of us don't realize just how much mental energy we spend on distractions until they're gone. It's not that you're less intelligent or motivated than the people around you, it's just that you're more distracted!

Once you find your focus increasing, you'll naturally find your creativity start to awaken as well. Creative thought is one of the most advanced functions your brain can perform, and so it's very difficult to have good ideas when you're constantly worried, distracted, and multitasking. However, even the most mentally disciplined can't be creative all the time. When you find your mind starting to wander, this is an indicator that your creative flow isn't working. The more vulnerable you are to distractions, the more tired your brain probably is. Rather than giving in to distractions, there are two directions you can take when you find yourself unable to sit and focus on your work.

One direction is to **stimulate your mind.** Perhaps your creativity isn't flowing because you just don't have the ideas or the information that you need to complete the task at hand. Rather than giving in to distractions, schedule yourself some downtime to engage with stimulating media or talk with an interesting person. Give your brain another direction to move in, another idea to consider, and new information to file away. Sometimes, the further removed your downtime activity is from your current project, the better. Sometimes chaining yourself to your desk and *making* yourself work is good for you. It forces you to clear away distractions and just get to work. But while you can make yourself work, you can't make yourself create. If you're not in the right mindset, then you're not in the right mindset. Learn how to incorporate stimulating brain activities into your daily routine to keep your brain active and versatile. This isn't procrastination or distraction. This is feeding your brain with new ideas.

That being said, sometimes wandering thoughts are really just what happens when our brains are trying to take the easy way out. You know that worktime is coming, and all of a sudden, you're unable to focus. Oh no, guess I need to take a break after all…

Don't let your brain do this to you. This is where Spartan discipline can serve you in your creative endeavors. If you have a project due today, then you just have to sit down at your desk and make yourself do it. If you want to become a great writer, then eventually you have to sit down and write, even if you don't feel like it. Very few of us feel energized and inspired when we sit down to work in the morning. But after a few minutes of staring foggily at the computer screen, your brain will slowly start to settle in and focus. Before you know it, the ideas are flowing and you've burned through an hour of highly productive, focused work. The more disciplined you are, the easier it will be for your brain to switch from morning relaxation to morning work. This is why the Spartans scheduled their lives so rigidly. They didn't give themselves another option. If now is time to train, then I'm going to sit here and train until it's time to do something else. This is why all of us could benefit from some tight scheduling as well. If it's time to work, make yourself sit and work until it's time to do something else. If you have regular breaks scheduled into your day, you'll also find it much easier to power through moments of laziness or avoidance because you can see the finish line. *Ok, let me just do this for an hour* is much more motivating than *Oh my god, it's only 9:30…lunch couldn't come fast enough!*

This is why many people find success in blocking out their first half hour of work answering emails or other notifications. Answering notifications is typically pretty mindless work, but the very mindless nature of it wakes up your brain and gently helps it to start thinking about work. It's like stretching before working out. It's a way to warm up the creative muscles in your brain so that when you do dive into your first task of the day (which, ideally, will be the most important) your mind is awake, focused, and fully committed to completing the task at hand.

The other direction you can move in when you find yourself battling distraction is to **relax**. This can be something physical like stretching, lighting a candle, or taking a walk. It can be something mental like meditation or putting on some music. Sometimes your brain is just tired. Trying to stuff it with more stimulation isn't necessarily going to help you in the moment, and neither is forcing it to keep going. Even the most hardened Spartan would care for his body in moments of sickness or recovery from a major injury. He would still go out and train, but he probably wouldn't push himself as hard as he would when he was healthy. At some point, pushing yourself beyond your limits does more harm than good.

If you're feeling burned out and overwhelmed, cancel whatever activities you had planned for your breaktime. Use it to stretch, sit in silence, or find a quiet place to meditate. If you're feeling sick, highly stressed, or deeply distracted by important personal matters, don't be afraid to extend your break times. Take a half an hour instead of your usual 15 minutes. Do something pleasing to the senses like drink a warm cup of tea or wrap yourself in a cozy sweatshirt. If your brain is really agitated or distracted, sometimes the only remedy is to fully relax it. Think of this as a kind of reboot for your mental energy, a way for your brain to fully process all of the thoughts and emotions clogging up your ability to think. Once all distractions have faded away, then when you go back to your work, you'll find yourself feeling much more energized and clear-headed.

Depending on the nature of your work, your own personality, and your own biorhythms, you may even want to schedule stimulating or relaxing activities for different break times throughout the day. For example, imagine that you're a "morning" person. You feel your most fresh and energized when you first wake up in the morning. If you're this kind of person, then take advantage!

As soon as you sit down at your desk at 9am, get to work on your most important task of the day. After an hour's work, take 15 minutes to do something stimulating like read or listen to a podcast. Jump right back into work for another hour. At this point it's 11:15. Take 15 minutes or even a half an hour to eat something. Jump back into work for another hour. At this point, we'll say it's 12:45pm. This is the time in the afternoon when your energy starts to fade. When you take your next break, now is the time to do something relaxing. If at all possible, stretch or even do a 15 minute yoga routine. Meditate. Simply sit at your desk with your head back and your eyes closed. Though it might feel counterintuitive to relax your mind when you're feeling tired and foggy-headed, that's exactly the right time to relax your mind.

Brain fog is a sign that your brain is overworked and overwhelmed. In order to clear it, you have to remove intense stimulation from your environment and give your mind a moment to rest and fully recharge. For the rest of the afternoon, fill your breaks with relaxing activities, and regulate your final half-hour of work to answering emails or other notifications before packing up to go home.

This is only an example routine, and the routine that works for you may look very different. This illustrates how routine can help to stimulate your creative mind and give your brain the fuel it needs to remain energized and focused throughout the day. In the modern world, we often look at discipline, routine, and structure as the opposite of creativity, but the Spartans understood that you can't be truly creative without discipline. A tight schedule, tailored to your specific mental, environmental, and professional needs, will free your brain from the mental energy of deciding what to do next. From the moment you start your workday to the moment you finish it, you'll have a plan in place that's designed to care for your brain in the best way possible.

Your routine is your brain's best friend. At first, you'll have to do some experimenting to find what works for you and your job. But once you've found a work routine that works for you, you'll find yourself far more productive than you would ever have believed possible. Don't look at your routine as something rigid or imprisoning. Instead, look at it as a foundation on which your brain can lean, freeing up your mental energy for the work that's most important to you.

Chapter 6:

Conquer Your Goals and Create the Life of Your Dreams

You've found your north star, or your life's purpose. You've started taking steps to eliminate distractions and improve your focus. You're even employing routines and activities into your daily life to stimulate your creative energy. Now it's time to put all of this together and start living the life you've always wanted to live.

The final step in the journey of success is cultivating self-empowerment. A Spartan never doubted, not for one second, that he had the skill and strength he needed to succeed in battle, no matter the odds. Once you've reached that same level of self-reliance and self-confidence, you'll be nearly unstoppable when it comes to achieving your goals.

However, it's one thing to discover your life's purpose and set long-term goals, and quite another to actually motivate yourself to achieve them. Discovering your north star is a critical first step, but you must find within yourself the motivational drive that you need to implement the necessary changes to start accomplishing what you want to accomplish. Too often, people do the hard work of reflecting on what they truly want from life, creating a list of sub-goals that they need to accomplish in order to fulfill their life's purpose, and then stop there. They make the plan, but they never actually take the first step, becoming more and more frustrated with themselves as the months and years roll by.

The essential ingredient between planning and action is motivation. This is the last mental hurdle that you need to overcome in order to become truly mentally resilient. Once you've mastered how to get and stay motivated, there will be nothing you can't achieve. Though the tricks people employ to motivate themselves vary from person to person, there are a few common mental exercises you can try to push yourself from thinking about your goals to actually achieving them (Joel Brown (Founder of Addicted2Success.com), 2013).

Create Reality-Based Goals

To become motivated, the goals you set for yourself must be attainable. At least, your sub-goals must be. There's nothing more demoralizing than setting yourself targets that are too high for you to achieve.

The most common way that people destroy their motivation is by setting goals that are too vague. Wanting to be "skinny" or "wealthy" are impossible goals to achieve because they aren't specific. How do you know when you've achieved "skinny"? How much wealth makes you "wealthy"?

When setting goals, be as specific as you possibly can. You don't want to be skinny, you want to lose 20 pounds or achieve a healthy BMI for your height and gender or be able to bench 250 lbs. These goals are much easier to work toward because there's a specific end in sight. Perhaps you don't want to be wealthy per se, you just want to be debt free. Instead of trying to play the lottery or surfing the Internet for get-rich-quick schemes, set yourself the goal of paying off your credit cards within a certain amount of months or years. Once you've set yourself an achievable goal with a measurable benchmark, then the small steps that you need to take in order to get there will become more obvious. More importantly, it will be much easier to get yourself to go to the gym or start saving money because the targets that you've set for yourself actually seem attainable.

The three most common obstacles to achieving personal goals are time, money, and ability. In the words of Brian Tracy, there are no unrealistic goals, just unrealistic deadlines. Often, we find ourselves failing to achieve our goals because we simply didn't give ourselves enough time to achieve them. Unexpected changes or challenges can take up time as well. Don't allow changes in schedule to derail your entire project. If something takes more time than expected, simply adjust your deadlines accordingly. Next time, you'll be better prepared (Whitbourne, 2018).

The same can be said for money. Often, we either underestimate how much the achievement of our goals is going to cost, or we look at the cost and give up, deciding that our goal wasn't realistic after all. But look at unexpected costs the same way you would view any other challenge, and look at funding your projects as just one step on your motivational map. If you're going to need a certain amount of money in order to get this started or to achieve the next step, then your next task must be to find a way to raise that money. Finding a way to fund your project is just another step on your journey. It's not a sign that what you're trying to accomplish isn't worth pursuing (Whitbourne, 2018).

Finally, we often assign ourselves targets that are too high because we overestimate our skills, talents, or abilities. Whether your goal is to retile the bathroom or win an Olympic medal, you have to start wherever you are right now. If you've never retiled a bathroom before, then you're going to have to plan yourself time to learn, practice, and watch others. You're going to have to expect the unexpected. You have no idea what challenges may arise because you have no experience. That's ok! It's all part of the journey. Don't get frustrated with yourself when you realize that you're in over your head. Instead, take a moment to do the necessary studying, practicing, and training that you need to improve your skill set. Don't beat yourself up for not being skilled, experienced, or talented enough to achieve what you want to achieve. Instead, bend your energy toward attaining the skills and experiences that you need to accomplish your goals (Whitbourne, 2018).

Build a Motivation Map

Once you've set yourself a clear, specific list of goals you want to achieve, you then have to build yourself a road map to guide you toward the achievement of those goals. Build a different map for each different area of your life that you wish to change. Health, finances, career, relationships, social life, or any other area of self-improvement should each have its own separate motivation map.

At the bottom of the page, write the word "Start." This is where you are right now in your life. At the top of the page, write the goal, whatever it is. Now it's time to fill the space between with all of the little steps and benchmarks you'll need to overcome in order to reach that final goal. Think of your motivation map as your life's itinerary. This is the bigger "schedule" that you're going to follow until you've achieved your goal, following the north star of your life's purpose the entire way through.

For example, if your current sub-goal is to change your career to something that you are more passionate about, then your first step might be updating your resume, or even going back to school. The next step might be searching for job postings, or gaining the relevant experience you need to start applying for the jobs that you really want. It doesn't matter how many steps lie between where you are now and the end goal. What's important is giving you a clear view of the path you need to take in order to turn your dream into a reality.

Celebrate Every Achievement

Every time you achieve a small step on your road map, celebrate that as a victory of its own. This is why some kind of physical or digital version of your map is important. As you accomplish each of the smaller steps on your list, you can physically cross them off or otherwise follow your progress. Watching yourself get closer and closer to achieving your goal is a huge motivator. Without a clear view of your path and your progress along it, it's easy to lose motivation or convince yourself that you aren't getting anything done. Following your progress along your motivation map will show you all the things that you *can* do and that you *are* capable of achieving, making your end goal seem ever more attainable.

Keep Your Eyes on the Road

This is where your north star comes in. As you're driving along your motivational road, progressing steadily closer to your goal, there are going to be times that are difficult and painful. There are going to be obstacles and setbacks. There are going to be times when you actually feel like you're *losing* progress, or when you feel utterly stuck, unable to move forward to achieve the next item on your list. It's at these moments when it becomes tempting to give up. Keeping your mind focused on your north star will remind you *why* you want to achieve this goal in the first place. It will remind you of what it is you're fighting for, and will therefore remind you that all the pain and frustration you're experiencing right now is worth it.

Visualization

Keep your motivational road map or progress marker with you where you can reference it at all times. If you're trying to lose weight, looking at the numbers on the scale or seeing a visual image of the numbers go down is extremely empowering. When companies see their growth on bar graphs or other charts, it makes everyone feel motivated to take on even bigger and more difficult projects. Whatever your goal may be, find a way to keep track of your progress in a clear, visual way. Hang your motivational map on your wall or employ the use of a progress-tracking app to give you a little boost of inspiration whenever you're feeling like giving up.

Don't Allow Detours to Derail You

The true test of our discipline and motivation comes when challenges appear. When you first make your motivational map, you have no idea what obstacles or life changes might arise to complicate the path toward the achievement of your goal. The reality is that unexpected changes and challenges are inevitable. Very rarely do we sail smoothly toward the achievement of our goals without any difficulties or setbacks. It's ok to make changes or modifications to your plan. It's ok to move your deadlines or adjust your expectations midway through the journey.

What you don't want is for these unexpected challenges to throw you off the path entirely. Even big changes like loss, health concerns, or losing a job don't mean that you can't continue forward with the accomplishment of your dreams. You may have to switch priorities for a while, or find an alternate route to achieving your goal when you find the path ahead blocked off. You may just have to grit your teeth and power through this moment of hardship. Look at these changes and challenges like a Spartan. Look at them as opportunities to get stronger, acquire more skills, and gain more glory. After all, the more difficult it is to achieve your goal, the more impressive its achievement actually is.

Common Obstacles and How to Avoid Them

Before you can make any real change to your life, you have to start believing that change is possible. When you finally do take the first step toward achieving your goals, you're inevitably going to run into all kinds of challenges and obstacles. The nature of the challenges you face will vary depending on who you are and what you want to achieve, but there are some common pitfalls that many people experience when they start embarking seriously on their journey toward achieving their dreams (Morin, 2020).

"Someday" Is Not a Deadline

You'll never find "someday" on a calendar or schedule because "someday" doesn't exist. Stop telling yourself that you'll achieve your goals "someday" or "eventually," because if you do this, then you'll never actually get motivated enough to accomplish them. If your goal is truly important to you, then you need to set yourself a timeline. Maybe you can't take the first step today, but set aside time tomorrow or next week or even next month. Choose an actual date on which to perform each task on your motivational plan. You can even set deadlines to coincide with the achievement of specific targets or expected life changes. For example, you can tell yourself that you'll start applying for promotions once your child starts school. But if you tell yourself that you'll apply for that promotion "eventually," you'll find every excuse in the book to push it off.

You're Never Going to Feel Ready

If you wait until you feel ready to start something, you're never going to start. Sudden bursts of inspiration and motivation are rare, and they don't last very long. This is where Spartan discipline can help you to get yourself started. Commit to the schedules and deadlines you set for yourself. No matter how uncomfortable you feel or how much you want to do something, sometimes you have to just roll up your sleeves and get started. Push through the initial discomfort. You'll never regret it.

Anticipate Rough Patches

Though visualizing yourself being capable and successful is important, don't convince yourself that nothing is going to go wrong. Difficulty and challenges are inevitable, whether you're trying to get out of debt, lose weight, or start a business. Some days will be hard. *Really* hard. If you know and accept that going in, those rough patches are less likely to push you off course.

NASA astronauts are actually encouraged to think about all the things that might go wrong when they're training for a launch. This might sound anxiety-inducing, but the logic behind it is to encourage the astronauts to make a plan for how they're going to handle the challenges and obstacles they might encounter while they're in space. That way, when something inevitably *does* go wrong, they aren't frozen with panic or fear. They already know what they're going to do when disaster happens, and so when faced with disaster, they simply do what they planned to do to fix the problem.

You may want to do something similar when setting your own goals. Think of everything that could possibly go wrong, and make a plan for how you're going to deal with those challenges if they appear. That way, when something does go wrong, you can confidently fall back on your disaster-management plan instead of panicking or getting discouraged.

Embrace Mistakes

You will encounter a number of setbacks along your journey, but making mistakes isn't one of them. Mistakes are necessary for learning. Making mistakes means that you're experimenting and trying something new. Expect that you're going to mess something up at some point. When you do make mistakes, don't beat yourself up or try to deny them. Instead, take responsibility, accept the consequences, and learn what you can from your mistake. Next time, you'll handle the same situation with much more competence and skill.

Make Your Goal a Priority

Whatever your goal is, it's the most important thing in your life. More important than watching Netflix or hanging out with friends. But implementing change in your life means making time to implement those changes. This is going to be uncomfortable at first.

Whether you're trying to work out more or find a new job, you're going to have to schedule yourself time to go to the gym or send out applications. That means that certain daily activities from your old routine are either going to have to be moved or eliminated altogether. This is where timelines, deadlines, and daily schedules are your friend. Rather than waking up every morning trying to convince yourself to go to the gym, simply set yourself a schedule. Monday, Wednesday, and Friday from 6-7am you're going to the gym. Period. No whining. No excuses. If the goal of becoming stronger or healthier is really important to you, then it's more important than spending an extra hour lazing around in bed. If staying out late is going to stop you from getting enough sleep to wake up early, then you're going to have to stay in. Make your goal, and all the actions necessary to achieve it, the most important things in your life. Take yourself and your dreams seriously.

Expect Hardship

Tell yourself, "I can do this." Don't tell yourself, "This will be easy." It won't be easy. At least, it usually won't be. Telling yourself that something is going to be easy is setting yourself up for failure. When the task before you becomes unexpectedly difficult, you aren't going to be in the right mental space to handle it. Tell yourself instead that it doesn't matter how hard the next step is. Tell yourself that you're tough enough to take it, no matter what hardships or discomforts come your way.

Don't Rely on Results

Monitoring your progress is a great motivator, but don't rely on the achievement of benchmarks to motivate you. Sometimes it takes longer than expected to hit a certain target or reach a certain milestone. Unexpected challenges or life changes can extend our timelines or even set us back. If you rely too much on results to keep you moving forward, then you might find yourself giving up too early. Just because you haven't hit your desired targets doesn't mean that your time and efforts were wasted. Every action that you take toward the accomplishment of your goal is worthy and worth it. Sticking to your schedule makes you stronger. Pushing through difficult times and unexpected challenges gives you experience. It teaches you about your own limitations. It makes you stronger, wiser, and more determined. Just because something took longer than expected to achieve doesn't mean it wasn't worth achieving. Impatience is the enemy of change.

Get Out of Your Own Way

Fear of success sounds like a paradox, but at one point or another, you're going to find yourself intentionally sabotaging yourself because you're actually afraid to achieve your goal. Fear of success can have a number of different root causes. Deep down, we may not believe that we're worthy of success. Perhaps we fear that someone will take it from us, or that we've somehow deluded ourselves into thinking the end is in sight. This is where self-empowerment and belief in yourself comes into play. You *are* worthy of success. And if an obstacle rises up just before you reach the finish line, then you'll just grit your teeth and power through it, the same as you've done with every obstacle that you've encountered before now.

Keep Your Sights At a Reasonable Level

Your north star is your life's purpose. There's no life's purpose too big or too unrealistic. However, the many sub-goals and the steps you take to achieve them underneath your north star should be achievable. If you set yourself targets that are too high, then it's easy to get discouraged and feel burned out. If you find yourself unable to reach the targets that you've set yourself, don't give up. Simply make some adjustments. Give yourself a timeline that's more reasonable. Maybe create an extra step toward making the money or acquiring the skills you need to achieve your goal. Keeping a realistic perspective on what you can actually achieve isn't sabotaging yourself. In fact, it's setting yourself up for success (Adams, 2016).

Stop Procrastinating

This might seem obvious, until you find yourself finding a number of "legitimate" reasons why you "can't" go to the gym today or get started on your project right now. Discipline is the antidote to procrastination, but it often takes a lot more strength than we first suppose. Get yourself into a "no-excuse" mindset. Achieving your goal is the most important thing. It's the number one priority. Therefore, nothing that comes up to stop you from doing what you need to do to achieve your goal is important. Don't accept any excuses, and don't view challenges or obstacles as "reasons" why you "can't" do what you need to do. Don't allow your brain to wiggle its way out of doing something that's just uncomfortable. Embrace the discomfort, and stop giving yourself reasons not to get to work (Krause, 2017).

Stop Thinking About the Future

The whole point of setting yourself timelines, deadlines, and strict daily schedules is so that you can stop thinking about the future and start thinking about right now. At some point, you have to stop dreaming and planning and start *doing.* Taking action means focusing on right now. Imagining the future can be inspiring and motivating, but it's no replacement for actually getting down to work. Allow yourself time every day or every week to plan, schedule, and adjust. Once your planning time is over, refocus your mind on the task at hand so that you can get to work (Krause, 2017).

Show Gratitude

Showing gratitude is a simple action, but it has huge benefits for your mindset. Gratitude keeps us humble, but it also keeps us content. Gratitude is what truly keeps us feeling comfortable in the face of discomfort, happy in the face of hardship, and content in the face of scarcity. There is no resilience without gratitude, and no true self-empowerment without recognizing all of the things that the people around you do to support you every single day.

If you're a science person, then you might be interested to know that gratitude isn't just a self-help concept. The Brain Opioid Theory of Social Attachment is a scientific theory that suggests long-term, positive social relationships in humans and other primates are partly driven by the presence of natural opioid molecules in the brain. In other words, positive social engagement has a soothing, healing, pain-eliminating effect on the brain that is comparable to opioid drugs like morphine (Maddaus, 2020).

Gratitude is the single best way to foster positive relationships with other people. Simply saying "thank you" goes a long way toward making someone else feel seen, valued, and respected. Think of gratitude as the social morphine for the pain of growth and change. Whatever hardships you face, whatever pain you embrace as part of your daily life, can be chemically and emotionally soothed by the simple act of expressing gratitude.

This might sound silly, but it's part of the Spartan philosophy as well. Gratitude is what the entire code of honor is based on. Remember, no Spartan was seen to be superior to anyone else. All Spartans were expected to work hard, fight hard, and support each other. Spartans trained as hard as they did to support each other as much as they could to improve themselves. Their philosophy of physical and mental discipline and the achievement of martial excellence was community based. They went out of their way to show respect and support for one another on a daily basis. There's no code of honor that isn't based, on some level, on gratitude.

So as you set out to achieve your dreams, make gratitude an essential part of your daily routine. This can take many different forms, but I've found two simple strategies that work particularly well for many different kinds of people. The first strategy is **a daily thank you.** Challenge yourself to say thank you at least once every single day. This might sound foolishly simple, but if you're like most people, you'll be astonished when you first begin this challenge to discover how easy it is to go an entire day without saying thank you even once. Observe how much better you feel, how much easier your relationships become, and how much more emotionally grounded you feel from saying these simple, powerful words just once every day.

The other strategy is to keep a **gratitude journal**. Every morning when you wake up or every night before you go to bed, simply write down three things that you are grateful for. These things can be vague ("I'm grateful that I'm healthy") or specific ("I'm grateful that my doctor's appointment today went smoothly"). They can be big ("I'm grateful that my wife's cancer is in remission") or small ("I'm grateful that there was no line at Starbucks this morning"). The actual items on your list don't matter. What matters is that you set aside time to acknowledge three things that have improved and warmed your life every single day. This is a very simple action, but taking the time to do this will make it much, much easier for you to face the pain and hardship of everyday life. Focusing on the things that are going right in your life gives you the necessary boost of confidence that you need to tackle the things that need to change.

Conclusion

The Spartans were some of the most feared and respected warriors in the ancient world. They accomplished feats in battle that other warriors would never believe possible. They faced odds that even the bravest men would run from without thinking. But these men (and women) weren't superhuman—they were mentally tough.

Now you, too, have all of the tools you need to achieve the same level of mental toughness as the Spartans before you. Though the ways in which you apply their philosophies may look very different, the underlying principles are the same. Discipline. Focus. Commitment. Gratitude. These are the skills that all humans need in order to achieve their dreams and push themselves to ever greater heights of success.

Remember, however, that mental toughness is a skill. As you begin working through the different sections of this book and applying the strategies included here to your own life, you're going to find it hard at first. That's ok. Embrace the hardship. Stop looking at pain and discomfort as a sign of weakness. Stop looking at hardship or mistakes as a sign of failure. And above all, stop measuring your success based on how comfortable and happy you are, and start measuring your success based on how close you are to living the life that *you* want to live.

With this book in hand, there's nothing that can get in the way of you achieving your goals and living your dreams. Are you afraid? That's ok, you have all the strategies you need to both embrace and use your fear to power your motivation. Is it hard? Painful? That's ok, too. As you build mental toughness, difficulty and pain will no longer be things you shy away from. In fact, these will be the things that you embrace as opportunities to become stronger, wiser, and more experienced.

It's this kind of resilience that will place you in a class above the rest. While others allow their fears, distractions, and discomforts to limit their abilities, you will shy away from nothing. There will be no challenge too daunting for you to tackle, no problem too complicated for you to solve. While others are lost, unsure of what they truly want from life or afraid to do what must be done to get it, you will be following your north star, secure in the knowledge that every step you take is worth it because it's bringing you that much closer to fulfilling your life's purpose.

Consider this book your primer, your Spartan training manual for achieving your goals. When life becomes difficult or when you feel like giving up, return to this book for guidance, inspiration, and motivation. Every single exercise or strategy in this book may not be a perfect fit for you, and that's ok. Feel free to adjust any suggestions or strategies in this book to fit your specific needs. Think like a Spartan now. Don't hesitate to get out there and do what must be done. The only thing that can hold you back from achieving your dreams now is you. You are the master of your own destiny.

References

Adams, R. L. (2016, November 21). *15 Bulletproof Strategies for Achieving Your Goals*. Entrepreneur. **https://www.entrepreneur.com/article/284783**

Babauta, L. (n.d.). *Why Fear of Discomfort Might Be Ruining Your Life : zen habits*. Zenhabits.Net. **https://zenhabits.net/discomfort-ruin/**

Daskal, L. (2020, February 6). *10 Smart Tips to Prevent Distractions and Sharpen Your Focus*. Inc.Com. **https://www.inc.com/lolly-daskal/10-smart-tips-to-prevent-distractions-and-sharpen-your-focus.html**

Deschene, L. (2015, January 24). *5 Ways to Push Through Discomfort to Reach Your Goals*. Tiny Buddha. **https://tinybuddha.com/blog/5-ways-to-push-through-discomfort-to-make-positive-change/**

Dixon, A. (2018, March 16). *Boost Your Creativity: 7 Ways to Be Insanely Creative on Demand*. WTD. **https://writetodone.com/boost-your-creativity/**

E. (n.d.). *The Spartan Military - Sparta: The Warrior State of Ancient Greece*. Erenow.Net.

https://erenow.net/ancient/sparta-the-warrior-state-of-ancient-greece/9.php

Fahkry, T. (2018, June 1). *Stop Resisting What Is Taking Place In Your Life And Embrace Everything As It Is.* Medium. **https://medium.com/the-mission/stop-resisting-what-is-taking-place-in-your-life-and-embrace-everything-as-it-is-e56f386c84e6**

Grenny, J. (2019, March 26). *How to Be Creative on Demand.* Harvard Business Review. **https://hbr.org/2019/01/how-to-be-creative-on-demand**

Gyatso, V. G. K. (n.d.). *What is the Mind?* Kadampa Buddhism. **https://kadampa.org/reference/mind**

Ho, L. (2019, August 25). *How to Find Your North Star.* Lifehack. **https://www.lifehack.org/847950/how-to-find-your-north-star**

Jarus, O. (2017, September 23). *History of Ancient Sparta.* Live Science. **https://www.livescience.com/32035-sparta.html**

Joel Brown (Founder of Addicted2Success.com). (2013, August 8). *Shirley Martin Wang.* Addicted 2 Success. **https://addicted2success.com/success-advice/6-fail-proof-ways-to-beat-your-unreachable-goals/**

K. (2014, March 12). *7 Badass Lessons You Learn From Spartans*. Thought Catalog. **https://thoughtcatalog.com/kyle-eschenroeder/2014/03/7-badass-lessons-you-learn-from-spartans/**

Kaipa, P. (2014, July 23). *What Wise Leaders Always Follow*. Harvard Business Review. **https://hbr.org/2012/01/what-wise-leaders-always-follo#:%7E:text=Wisdom%20is%20not%20about%20focusing,guidance%20helps%20simplify%20one's%20choices.**

Krause, W. (2017). *Seven Habits You Must Stop Doing If You Want to Achieve Your Dream Goal.* Medium.Com. **https://medium.com/thrive-global/7-habits-you-must-stop-doing-if-you-want-to-achieve-your-dream-goal-44d38592e575**

Lane, A. (2016, April 29). *12 Tips for Staying Focused and Avoiding Distraction at Work*. The Work Smarter Guide - Redbooth. **https://redbooth.com/hub/12-tips-for-staying-focused-and-avoiding-distraction-at-work/**

Maddaus, M. (2020, January 2). *Why gratitude is a superpower*. KevinMD.Com. **https://www.kevinmd.com/blog/2020/01/why-gratitude-is-a-superpower.html**

Mires, E. A. (2020, January 21). *How to Not Get Distracted: 10 Practical Tips to Sharpen Your Focus.*

Lifehack. **https://www.lifehack.org/articles/productivity/10-critical-tips-prevent-distraction-and-sharpen-your-focus.html**

Morin, A. (2020, February 6). *How to Overcome the 9 Most Common Obstacles That Prevent People From Living Their Dreams.* Inc.Com. **https://www.inc.com/amy-morin/9-things-that-will-prevent-you-from-reaching-your-goals-and-how-to-avoid-those-c.html**

N.G. (2020, February 5). *Bred for Battle—Understanding Ancient Sparta's Military Machine.* Nationalgeographic.Com. **https://www.nationalgeographic.com/history/magazine/2016/11-12/sparta-military-greek-civilization/**

Niederhofer, H. (2017, August 27). *4 Ways We Resist Life and Cause Ourselves Pain (And How to Stop).* Tiny Buddha. **https://tinybuddha.com/blog/4-ways-resist-life-cause-suffer-how-to-stop/**

Patel, D. (2018, December 12). *7 Proven Strategies for Overcoming Distractions.* Entrepreneur. **https://www.entrepreneur.com/article/324560**

Razzetti, G. (2019, October 8). *This Is the Reason Why People Resist Change.* Liberationist - Change Leadership. **https://liberationist.org/this-is-the-reason-why-people-resist-change/**

Rubarth, S. (n.d.). *Stoic Philosophy of Mind | Internet Encyclopedia of Philosophy*. Iep.Utm.Edu. **https://www.iep.utm.edu/stoicmind/#:%7E:text=As%20in%20contemporary%20cognitive%20science,states%20of%20the%20corporeal%20soul.**

T. (2019). *How to become creative on demand – Timely Blog.* Memory. **https://memory.ai/timely-blog/how-to-become-creative-on-demand**

Vilhauer, J. (2018). *Should You Feel the Fear and Do It Anyway?* Psychologytoday.Com. **https://www.psychologytoday.com/us/blog/living-forward/201806/should-you-feel-the-fear-and-do-it-anyway**

Whitbourne, S. K. (2018). *Three Obstacles to Reaching Your Goals and How to Conquer Each.* Psychologytoday.Com. **https://www.psychologytoday.com/us/blog/fulfillment-any-age/201801/3-obstacles-reaching-your-goals-and-how-conquer-each**

www.ingramcontent.com/pod-product-compliance
Ingram Content Group UK Ltd.
Pitfield, Milton Keynes, MK11 3LW, UK
UKHW041956190726
13854UKWH00005B/2018

9 798676 066185